Ho     Vin Customers

# How to Win Customers

## Using Customer Service for a Competitive Edge

JACQUES HOROVITZ

29

Pitman

HF
5415.5
.H6

24 SEP 1991

Pitman Publishing
128 Long Acre, London WC2E 9AN

A Division of Longman Group UK Limited

First published in French
*La Qualité de Service*
© InterEditions 1987

English translation first published in 1990
© Longman Group UK Ltd 1990

**British Library Cataloguing in Publication Data**

Horovitz, Jacques
How to win customers
1. Companies. Customer Services. Management aspects
I. Title II. La qualité de service. *English*
658. 812

ISBN 0-273-03288-7

All rights reserved; no part of this publication may be reproduced, stored in a retrieval system, or transmitted in any form or by any other means, electronic, mechanical, photocopying, recording or otherwise without either the prior written permission of the Publishers or a licence permitting restricted copying in the United Kingdom issued by the Copyright Licensing Agency, 33-34 Alfred Place, London WC1E 7DP. This book may not be lent, resold hired out or otherwise disposed of by way of trade in any form of binding or cover other than that in which it is published, without the prior consent of the Publishers.

Printed in Great Britain at The Bath Press, Avon

# Contents

# Preface

European companies, awakened by the success of their American and Japanese counterparts, have become increasingly conscious of service quality.

I am delighted by this new awareness and hope it will soon result in an reorganization of company structures and a universal adoption of quality policies.

Indeed, service quality has been the hallmark of our work at Club Med. Thirty-five years ago, we realized that service was the primary reason for our existence. Without relentless, company-wide dedication to providing customer-driven service, we would never have become the leader in our field.

We developed a rigorous service delivery policy which is now central to everything we do, whether it be the training of our staff, the building of our international villages, or the error hunt for 'zero defect'. This passion for service quality is closely linked to the implicit promise we make to all our members: happiness. Service quality is the onus of the entire organization. Employees, supervisors, managers, and all those who are in contact with the customer, must cooperate in a vast, organized error hunt which will only reach 'zero defect' if everyone involved in it acts with the same enthusiasm.

Buttressed by his double experience as teacher and practitioner, Jacques Horovitz echoes our priority in this book. He demonstrates that, in today's world, no company can survive without paying attention to the customer and to the quality of the service which it must provide.

The author has counselled Club Med on the integration of its service quality dimension. His vision will undoubtedly be useful in every business sector, including the product industry, as the many examples in this book demonstrate.

Getting to the heart of the matter, Jacques Horovitz illustrates the importance of quality as perceived by the customer. He discusses methods which will make it possible to surmount the difficulties in managing service quality and he does not hesitate to denounce the harmful consequences of non-quality (such as costs and poor reputation).

He reminds us of the role of communications, both internal and external, in the success of a service strategy and he explains in all its aspects in detail, from the welcome to advertising messages, and includes documentation and telephone behaviour.

In order to hold their own in markets which are increasingly competitive, companies will have to establish specific and detailed programmes focusing on quality. For this purpose, Jacques Horovitz describes ways to launch a service quality programme. By following the author's guidelines, the reader will be able to prepare a diagnosis regarding the status of service in his company, and, if need be, to improve or reorganize the quality policy.

At Club Med, we constantly remind ourselves that we must strive to satisfy the customer (after all, isn't the customer always right?) by anticipating his needs and responding to his expectations. Jacques Horovitz has been able to illustrate this attitude with relevant anecdotes.

Knowing that a dissatisfied customer will relate his dissatisfaction to eleven people, while a satisfied customer will only communicate his satisfaction to three, it is evident that a good manager will pay special attention to 'word of mouth'.

In this book, Jacques Horovitz gives vital information on conducting practical satisfaction surveys which should be the starting and finishing point of each company activity.

I do not want to reveal any more about the content of this book, but I would like to assure the reader that it offers an original approach to service quality. With its generous and effective themes, it will become an indispensable companion for managers at all levels in the conquest of zero defect, the real priority in today's competitive, international environment.

Gilbert Trigano
June 1987

# Acknowledgements

In way of acknowledgements, I would like to begin with two words borrowed from customer service:

**Hello**
To the reader who is interested in service quality and strategy.

**Thanks**
To the reader for sending me his comments, experiences and ideas.
To Danielle, who had faith in me.
To Charles, Mark and Dago, who read and reread my manuscript and commented on it.
To Marta, who typed and retyped the text to 'zero defect'.
To all the progress-oriented companies with whom I have spent time in the search for perfection, and who have called upon me to create, develop and reinforce their service quality policies.

I owe a special debt of gratitude to Club Med, that great service company which has always been in the forefront of quality. The GO (*'Gentil Organisateur'*) spirit, with its generosity and attentiveness permeates each member, from the CEO to the sailing instructor. Club Med sells the most intangible of services: happiness. Its goal is to provide 'zero defect' happiness for the GM *('Gentil Membre')*. Implementing a system to establish such an ambitious policy throughout the world has been a particularly interesting job for Club Med and for myself. The Club adopted the system and the positive results quickly became apparent. Club Med's achievement of 'zero defect' happiness should provide encouragement to other, more down-to-earth service providers. Spare auto parts dealers, data bank sales and restaurants will find the quest equally exciting and fulfilling.

So, to everyone in business, from large scale retailing to hotels, from insurance to computers, and steel manufacturing: Don't be afraid to seek 'zero defect' service . . . for your customers' sake.

I would also like to thank Peter Jones, Principal Lecturer of the Brighton Business School, for having read and commented on the English translation.

# Introduction

The battle for product quality took off when the Japanese launched their trade war against Europe and the United States. In 1981, American CEOs were still declaring that 80 per cent of their products were of better quality than Japanese products. However, 80 per cent of American consumers thought differently. The battle intensified with the introduction of concepts like 'zero failure', 'zero problem', 'zero deficiency' and 'zero defect'.

More recently, an offensive has been launched on the service front. Service before, during and after product sale, has become increasingly important, and not only in the product industry. Companies in the service industry, such as banks, insurance companies, transporters, travel agencies, government agencies, restaurants and catering services, are just a few types of businesses which have also become concerned with service quality.

The service war is all the more crucial in Western economies, because here services represent an increasing share of GNP (70 per cent in the United States, 67 per cent in the United Kingdom, 65 per cent in France, 56 per cent in West Germany).

As a result of the combined effects of telecommunications and computers, concern with service quality will soon be global. Indeed, these two technologies will create economies of scale in services, thus providing large, multinational service companies with opportunities to create new markets at the expense of small, independent companies. Competition will no longer be merely local or national, but international, maybe in future even planetary. Finally, it will become possible to reconcile the irreconcilable. Thanks to advanced technologies, mass production will co-exist with services adapted to individual customers, blending high-tech with high-touch.

Even while presented with these new opportunities, many companies continue to act as if they were in a market of scarcity. They do not seem to realize that international competition, in terms of service, will become tougher every day. A number of Japanese, Swiss, Singaporean, Dutch and Swedish companies on the other hand have accepted that the challenge of service excellence has now become worldwide. Many hotels, insurance companies, transporters, banks, data processing companies, consulting firms, travel agencies, tour operators, companies in such sectors as industrial cleaning, security, distribution, and food catering, have already spread across borders.

Service quality and product quality must, however, be managed differently. Service is intangible. Unlike products, which are manufactured before being sold and used, service is created and consumed simultaneously. A number of quality management techniques such as quality circles and the various error chasing methods developed by the industry, can be applied to service, but these alone are not enough to assure service quality.

In the product industry, quality management increases productivity by reducing waste and lowering production costs. In services, productivity is expressed through customer satisfaction, and is measured by increased sales.

The purpose of this book is to give managers of service companies and industrial companies, for whom service is a competitive weapon, the means to establish quality policies for the services they provide. In other words, it will try to point the way to service excellence.

Its objective is not to create an awareness of the customer's importance. This subject has already been explored in many books. *How to Win Customers* addresses the questions which naturally follow acceptance of the importance of the customer.

Methods do exist for managing the quality of services. I have tested them while assisting companies in diverse fields: restaurants, travel agencies, hotels, banks, large scale retailers, schools, computer services, spare parts dealers, and consulting firms.

The major principles upon which the quality of service depends, and those that will be developed in this book, can be summarized as follows:

- The customer is the only legitimate judge of service quality. His opinion is of vital importance.
- The customer determines the service excellence level and he always asks for more.
- Each company must formulate a promise which will enable it to satisfy its target clientele, while making money and distinguishing itself from the competition.

- Each company must manage the expectations of its customers, minimizing the difference between these expectation and company performance.

- Service promises must be converted into quality standards. Service quality is a very subjective idea. Nevertheless, it is possible to define precise standards.

- Strict discipline and constant vigilance are necessary to eliminate defects. In providing service, there is no middle road. The goal must be perfection: 'zero defect'. The quality of services can be improved by managing details.

- The quest for excellence demands a universal commitment. Everyone in the company must be involved, from the CEO to the newest employee.

Since every firm operates in its own distinctive universe, every effective service quality strategy will demand solutions unique to that universe. However, the principles stated above will be indispensable to the development of a service strategy, regardless of the internal and external circumstances of the company.

Each chapter concludes with a *Self-Diagnosis*, a series of questions designed to help the manager diagnose his present service quality policy. I hope these questions will provide guidance, and enable the reader to understand present conditions, to identify strengths and weaknesses, and to forge an action plan.

Finally, it may be a reflection of my allegiance to an 'old-school' way of doing things, but I typically use the masculine form of pronouns when referring to managers and customers. I certainly do not mean to imply that only males comprise either group. But since consistency is a major factor in managing service quality, I have opted to be true to my discipline. I trust that the ladies will find it in their hearts to be forgiving.

J.H.

# 1

# Quality and Service

This book is about understanding and managing service quality. Since service quality is a very subjective matter, it might be best to begin with a few definitions. Is there a single level of quality or are there several? How much does quality cost? What exactly do we mean by service?

## Quality

Quality is the *minimum level of service* which a firm chooses to provide in order to satisfy its *target clientele.* At the same time, it is the *degree of consistency* the firm can maintain in providing this pre-determined level of service.

### The level of service

In the world of services, quality does not necessarily mean luxury, supremacy or 'top of the line'. Management must first of all identify the level of service to which the company will aspire. A service reaches its degree of excellence when it meets the expectations of its target clientele, regardless of how that clientele is defined. If one customer segment wants a repairman to visit within three days, there is no need to provide a repairman within three hours. Dependent upon the target clientele in question, three days and three hours may be equally valid levels of excellence. A level of service should correspond to the values for which the customer is willing to pay.

### The target clientele

The target clientele is the one which, by its expectations and/or needs, dictates the level of service to be provided. Today, industrial and consumer markets are more and more fragmented by an ever increasing diversity of customers. A student has by no means the same expectations from a stay in an hotel than, for instance, a businessman. When buying a Fiesta one does not expect the same level of service that a BMW buyer expects. A law firm seldom demands the same quick repair time for its laser printer as a firm of architects.

Faced with the multiplicity of needs, each service must choose a target clientele. Yielding to the temptation to furnish a little bit of satisfaction to everyone is the surest way to failure.

## Consistency

Consistency is the third parameter of quality. It demands maintenance of the same level of excellence every day and everywhere. Guests cannot be received more cordially in the morning than in the afternoon. A restaurant chain cannot serve good food in one part of town and mediocre food in another. Conformity to standards is the aspect of service quality management which is most difficult to maintain.

The more dispersed a service distribution network is or the longer the chain of intermediaries, the greater the danger of deviating from a level of excellence.

Companies which sell through distributors, such as insurers, microcomputer firms, or tour operators, have an even more difficult job: to maintain their service quality towards these distributors and help them every day and everywhere to provide a high level of quality to the eventual customer.

In the same way, the more the quality of a service depends upon employee behaviour, the greater the risk of non-conformity. The main advantage of an automatic teller, for example, is that it is never in a bad mood.

Whether human behaviour has a major or insignificant effect on a service, whether or not the service is delivered through numerous locations or intermediaries, the objective must always be to reduce the gap between the service actually provided and the targeted level of excellence. Long-term success can only be guaranteed by constant and consistent monitoring of every phase of the delivery programme.

Disney theme parks are a model of consistency in the excellence of their ability to deliver quality service. The service is equally commendable whether one visits Mickey Mouse on the east coast or west. But the Disney success does not just happen. It is the result of comprehensive and consistent planning, training, monitoring and fine-tuning.

## Service

Service consists of all the supports which the customer expects, beyond the basic product or service, consistent with the price, image and reputation involved. The buyer of a Mercedes expects a certain number of basic service features during and after the actual purchase, i.e., an extended test drive, a personalized reception, tailored credit, fast repair or, even better, zero failure, plus the prospect of receiving a good price at trade-in time. When Hertz promotes its 'Number 1' position, it commits itself to great helpfulness, immaculate cars in perfect condition, and an immediate response to customer problems.

But service goes beyond friendliness or kindness. It is true that a smile is never superfluous. It is also true that a smile is 'visible' on the telephone. This smile must nevertheless be accompanied by the right information, it must connect the call to the right person and not expect the caller to 'hold' forever. Good service is a question of method and not merely one of simple courtesy.

If one hospital offers you a warm welcome but not much else, and another hospital treatment by an excellent though ill-tempered doctor, you would no doubt choose the latter. But why should you not have both?

Service does not mean servility. People tend to confuse them, which explains the well-known attitude of certain sales clerks in department stores who make one want to buy . . . elsewhere. A moment of pragmatism. Without the customer, there is no company and therefore, no job and no salary. And without service, there may be no customer.

Our parents, less spoiled than we are, were well aware of this when they worked long hours in their shops, sustained by a single truth: 'The customer is always right'.

### Service in a product industry

The service of products has two components: the degree to which the product is *hassle-free* and the *added value* the customer receives.

Beyond the fundamental usefulness and technical performance of the product itself, these factors are of equal interest to buyers of automobiles, bulldozers, computers, widgets and baby cribs.

*The hassle-free factor*

In addition to the price and technical performance of the product, the customer is interested in what his purchase is going to cost him in terms of time and effort. He looks at how easy it will be to

- get delivery and repair,
- receive an error-free invoice,
- operate the device,
- understand how the product works,
- use it at full efficiency,
- efficiently contact the right person in case of a problem,
- get rid of or resell the old machine, etc.

He also assesses the monetary costs connected with obtaining and using the product:

- transportation
- installation
- maintenance
- downtime

A properly tuned service quality policy aims to minimize the extra costs and efforts incurred by the customer. The objective is to achieve zero-hassle.

A happy customer is the one whose computer work is taken care of when his computer is under repair; who, thanks to a confidential telephone number, can submit a problem or an idea to the right person, have his old equipment removed and receive help with the new equipment during the start-up phase.

Not all buyers demand the same degree of hassle-freedom. Some choose to pay a high price for total service, others prefer to pay less and take on part of the service themselves. Digital Equipment Company (DEC), which has become a leading player in the world of computers in less than fifteen years, understands this principle very well. It offers a variety of service programmes, from the all-inclusive (everything done for you), to simply providing parts (do-it-yourself).

*The added-value factor*

The smart customer also looks for added value. He already understands the technical performance of the product. His choice of supplier will depend on less tangible considerations.

There are different kinds of added value. The *social status* of ownership is an important one. A Mercedes appeals to the businessman who wants to present an image of affluence and respectability. The Porsche meets the sporty playboy's need for prestige. An IBM computer offers the 'psychological' guarantee of a market-leader product. Macintosh attracts the 'hands-on' user, the innovator, the entrepreneur.

Added value can take the form of *problem-solving assistance*. By using this approach, a small American can maker, Crown Cork and Seal, beat the giants at their own game. The firm works closely with its customers to design and develop packaging adapted to individual needs; lightweight, less expensive and/or more suitable for merchandising. Problem-solving assistance is also encountered in high performance banks; each customer can invest his funds according to his needs, his means and his hunches.

Added value can include *financial support*, i.e., help in securing credit, easy payment terms, arranging the sale of old equipment or material.

It can be built around *after-sale support*, i.e., training, repair, guarantees, spare parts availability, continuity of the line, technical updating.

Finally, added value can mean *speed and/or flexibility*, i.e., speed in delivery or production, possibility of modifying an outstanding order.

A service policy, associated with a product, can therefore be analysed based on two parameters, the degree to which it is hassle-free and the added value. Figure 1.1 will provide a convenient way to track the service aspect during the various sales stages.

A company must define its priorities before it can develop a service policy to supports its product. For example, if a company chooses to distinguish itself by promoting a hassle-free policy before, during and after sale, it must provide the customer with effective service personnel, user-friendly documentation, start-up assistance, quick and complete delivery, error-free invoicing with clear references, minimum cost for maintenance, repair and down-time.

| | before sale | at installation | after sale |
|---|---|---|---|
| degree of being hassle-free | | | |
| added value | | | |

*Figure 1.1 The service dimensions of a product*

## Service in service industries

Unlike products, services have little or no tangibility. Services exist only in human experience. In most cases, the customer of a service cannot express his degree of satisfaction until after consumption. Product services can be conveniently divided into two components: the extent to which the product is hassle free and the added values obtained by the purchase of the product.

Service in service industries also consists of two dimensions: the *basic features* sought by the customer and *the service experience* at the time(s) of consumption.

### *Basic service features*

When a customer reserves a hotel room, he is buying rest. When he buys an insurance policy, he is seeking some form of financial security. Everything which accompanies the basic service becomes important. A play will only entertain if the seat is comfortable. On the other hand, a restaurant which aims for fast table turnover cannot satisfy the diner who has come to relax.

There is a modicum of service that any airline passenger or fast-food purchaser expects to receive. The airline passenger expects to arrive at a selected destination. The fast-food customer expects to receive a bag or tray containing something to eat. These are the basic services features involved in each transaction. History is replete with examples where even basic dividends could not be delivered by companies supposedly doing business in the service sector. Fortunately, history also records examples where basic services, when orchestrated in an innovative manner, can provide a service that is greater than the sum of the parts.

All airline tickets look pretty much the same. Most hotels look alike. But it was a unique combination of these elements, wrapped in a finely tuned service policy that Jan Carlson credits for the tremendous success of Scandinavian Airlines (SAS). The company began by identifying the businessman as its target audience. It then rescheduled flights, added a business class, a special waiting lounge, luggage check-in service at the hotel and efficient credit card procedures to address the specific needs of the businessman. The results are history.

*The consumer experience*

Service in service industries can have a major impact on the consumer's experience and therefore determine his degree of satisfaction. An experience will be pleasant or unpleasant, according to a variety of factors, including, but not limited to:

- selection;
- availability;
- ambience;
- attitude of the service staff (friendliness, courtesy, helpfulness, the initiatives) during the sale and while the service is being performed;
- risk perceived in choosing the service, which can be linked to the company's image and reputation;
- other customers;
- speed and accuracy of responses given to questions;
- reaction to complaints;
- personalization of services.

When selling a service, the customer's first contact is particularly important. The location, staffing and procedures of a check-in desk often leave one with a lasting impression of a hotel.

The first contact between the customer and the company is even more important when the service will demand multiple contacts. A hotel guest, for example, encounters a room clerk, a bellman, a chambermaid, a barman. Each of these early contacts must be successful. If the early ones are unsuccessful, there may be no later ones. The integrated nature of the two components is illustrated in Figure 1.2.

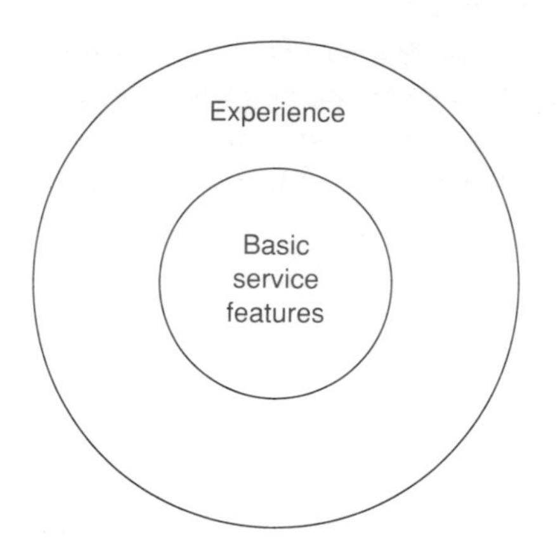


*Figure 1.2 The service dimensions of a service.*

When customers were asked to rate the aspects that influenced their choice of department stores, they gave the following answers, in order of importance:

1. The quality of the welcome; the friendliness of the personnel, the information desks, the signs, the ease of finding things and the advice from knowledgeable sales people.
2. Convenience; facility of access, easy circulation, purchase transaction speed, rest facilities, lighting and ventilation, festive atmosphere, the 'pleasure' of buying.
3. Choice; the availability and diversity of the items for sale.

The quality of the welcome proved to be twice as important as convenience and choice. Price and selection were secondary considerations. Welcome and convenience are perceived through a number of features (lighting and decoration) and from the experiences (atmosphere, circulation) which surround the act of buying. This is not very surprising. Why would one shop at a department store if not for the pleasure of the eyes, the ears and the other senses? The customer can find lower prices in discount stores and more personalized advice in boutiques.

Service can be equally important in banking and leisure industries. Can anyone resist the banker who offers a cup of coffee in the privacy of an attractive office?

Club Med owes its success more to the fact that it offers the opportunity to make new friends, an easy going atmosphere and freedom of choice in sports activities. Its magnificent beaches and sumptuous buffets are less significant.

Quality is the level of service which a company chooses to attain in order to satisfy its target clientele. It is also the degree to which the company succeeds in conforming to this level of excellence. Service is composed of all the aspects which surround the act of buying. It is measured in terms of hassle freedom and added value for products, and in terms of basic service features and the customer's experience(s) for a service.

## Self-diagnosis

If your company is product oriented:

a) Make a list of the present service dimensions:
   - the degree of hassle freedom (before, during and after the sale)
   - the added value (before, during and after the sale).

b) Can you see other possibilities?

c) Do your competitors offer more?

d) Do the dimensions you listed have different levels of importance for the various segments served?

e) Do you always comply with these levels and to what degree?

If your company is service oriented:

a) Make a list of the present service dimensions:
   - the basic service features
   - the experience.

b) Can you see other possibilities?

c) Do your competitors offer more?

d) Do the dimensions you listed have different levels of importance for the various segments served?

e) Do you always comply with these levels and to what degree?

# 2

# The Importance of Service Quality

## Quality for the customer

Consumer needs and aspirations for service quality are in constant evolution. Consumer studies show that customers are increasingly demanding. However, these findings do not give a full picture. The perception of quality varies from one customer to another. Suppliers often have different views on service quality than do their customers. Moreover, the quality of a service will be perceived differently according to whether the service is new or well established. The customer who has just discovered a service tends to be less critical in his judgment than the experienced user.

### Toward better quality

Service quality has become a major factor in many purchase decisions. The reasons are manifold. Competition has intensified in most businesses, from tourism to data processing, from banking to the glass industry. The customer is being tempted with greater and greater service diversity. Assuming parity in price, why should customers settle for a product offering less service?

Furthermore, the gluttonous consumer of the 1960s has been succeeded by a more selective and better informed gourmet. This trend has been exacerbated by the recent economic difficulties experienced by many Western nations and by a relative stagnation in consumer purchasing power. It is therefore not surprising that service forms an increasingly important factor in successful business strategies.

## Stepping up to something better

The customer's attitude toward service quality changes as he learns more about a product and/or raises his standard of living. In the beginning, the consumer is happy with a basic product, with stripped-down service and low price. Gradually, an awareness of quality grows until the consumer demands increased excellence. The demise of the British and European motorcycle industry in the face of Japanese engineering excellence is a typical example of this trend.

## The multiplicity of experiences increases the customer's expectations

A customer may want increased service quality because his buying behaviour has been influenced by the difference between what he receives at home and what he discovers in his travels. A businessman who spends time in Asia will be more demanding with regard to the service he receives in a domestic resort hotel than someone who has not experienced the charms of Asian hospitality. The tourist who has sampled the service quality of restaurants in Italy cannot resist comparisons with his favourite local restaurant.

The computer specialist who has experienced Digital Equipment's after-sale service in the United States, will not fail to compare it to analogous service in the UK.

As borders open and as trade becomes more international, quality expectations grow. To remain competitive companies must adopt standards to match their markets and stay abreast of what is happening in the rest of the service world.

The Japanese, for example, have a very strong tradition of courtesy which they do not fail to employ in their conquest of foreign markets. It gives them a competitive advantage in countries where the customer is not used to being treated with deference.

## Quality conceived and quality perceived are rarely the same

The superiority of a new service is always more evident to the inventor than it is to a potential customer. If the innovation deviates from the ordinary or if it amplifies a less tangible service, this gap widens. Every innovation encounters resistance to change, whether it offers a new dimension in the use of credit cards, automatic banking services or automatic train ticket dispensers.

It may be good to know that only two to three per cent of potential customers are generally willing to act as 'guinea pigs'. These few are usually followed by 'trend setters', who make up about 15 per cent of the market. The bulk of the market will come around much later.

Quality should therefore be the focal point of any campaign charged with communicating the comparative advantages of an innovation. Everything must contribute to reducing the risk perceived by the customer, i.e., brand image, reputation, guarantees, start-up assistance, user-friendly documentation, testimonials from satisfied users, ready availability of assistance personnel and even the direct involvement of top management.

## If you want something done – do it yourself.

Whether the product is new or well-established, some customers will compare service quality to the savings they can make by servicing themselves. The 'do-it-yourselfer' wants a repair service that only charges him for solving the problems that he cannot solve on his own. Some holidaymakers prefer to do most of their own planning and only use the travel agency for those details which they cannot arrange on their own.

## The advantage of being the leader, a dual-edged sword

There is a common belief that a Number 1 market position automatically creates a decisive competitive advantage. Asserting one's image and reputation can be advantageous in this context. It must be realized, however, that the more a company affirms its dominance, the more the customer will demand.

Number 1 benefits from a competitive advantage until the moment when, justified or not, it is perceived as being excessively dominant, arrogant or impersonal. When this 'leader syndrome' sets in, customers start to look elsewhere.

Companies like IBM, Xerox, British Airways, or Hertz, are well aware of this fact. They have all suffered because of it at one point or another. By constantly dominating, and by succeeding too well, the risk exists of irritating buyers who prefer a bit more 'modesty'.

## The meeting point

When prices are similar, the customer will choose the best service quality. When the quality is equivalent, the customer prefers the less expensive service. Figure 2.1 illustrates the meeting zone between the customer and supplier.

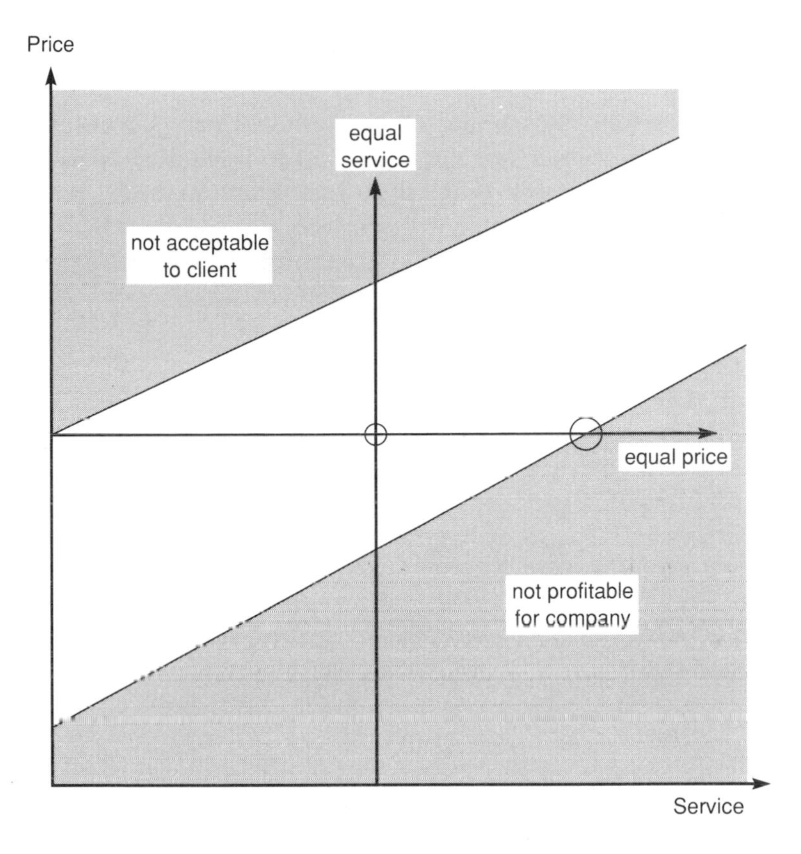


*Figure 2.1 Meeting points between customer and supplier*

## The importance of symbols and information

The perception of quality is influenced by the symbols surrounding the product. For example, fish always appear fresher when displayed on a bed of crushed ice. The ambience of an advertising agency's waiting room and the appearance of reception personnel often serve as a clue to the creativity of the entire organization. The same factors are also strong indications of how the agency treats its customers.

Verbal and non-verbal signs can play an important role in packaging a service, i.e., smiling to express pleasure at seeing the client, calling him by name, eye contact in conversation. All these signs can contribute to a quality image.

Information can also have a considerable effect on the manner in which quality is perceived. An intrinsically mediocre service can sometimes be excused if the user's perception is affected by an explanation of the reasons for the poor quality. When people waiting in line are told the reason for their wait, their aggravation is often tempered. This does not mean that a nice tune should have the responsibility of keeping telephone customers amused while they are holding. It is preferable to prepare a message which is appropriate to the service and to the customer, i.e., travel information for a tourist agency, or an explanation software innovations for a microcomputer manufacturer. The bottom line is simple: there is no substitute for a speedy, thorough answer.

## The more intangible the service, the greater the importance of tangible reference points

The customer may have to refer to tangible elements in order to judge the quality of a service. The more complex and intangible the service is, the more the user will rely on immediately measurable criteria, in particular:

- the physical appearance of the place and the people (a doctor's competence is often judged by the neatness of his waiting room);
- the price (the demand for quality generally increases in proportion to price);
- the risk perceived (the customer who receives little information and assistance from the outset, or who must buy without a guarantee, will perceive a lesser quality in the service even when such perception is objectively erroneous).

Where a product is evaluated in terms of its tangible and physical characteristics (the number of rooms in a house, its location, insulation and/or amenities, for example), a service is more often appreciated for intangible factors (the experience of past customers, the warmth of the welcome, the clarity of the information or the credibility of the company).

## Service quality is determined by customers' opinion

Companies often misjudge the customer's opinion. Absorbed by the technical performance of their products and ignorant of the real motivations for buying, companies tend to adopt unsuitable service quality policies. For example, a great number of firms promise a particular response time in case of machine failure, while the client is primarily concerned with knowing whether a replacement unit will be immediately available.

To maintain the level of excellence, it is essential to know what the customer's expectations are. The holidaymaker is, for instance, purchasing freedom from hassle. A supplier may be marketing education, but the customer is buying practical training. When the agency is selling advertising, the customer is buying sales. When the producer is promoting a musical comedy, the spectator is buying entertainment.

## Nearly-total service quality does not exist

When the customer evaluates service quality, he does not dissect it into components. He judges it as a whole. He forms an overall impression and seldom remembers the relative success of specific aspects.

Even more unfortunate is that the customer tends to focus on the weakest link in the quality chain. He then blames the entire service for the faults of the single ineffective link.

It is therefore essential in a service quality policy to ensure the utmost congruence among the elements. Whatever is offered, be it a product or a service, it will be judged on every aspect of its performance. A deficiency in any one area can result in failure for the entire system. That's why nearly-total service quality does not exist.

It is pointless to serve a sumptuous meal on a paper table cloth, to sell a sophisticated quartz watch without proper instructions, or a high-tech telephone system without at least offering to give technical assistance. As products and services become available on an international scale, the congruence of the quality becomes an even more important, competitive factor. If a company refuses to offer a certain service, a competitor may be waiting to capitalize on the refusal and develop its own competitive edge.

Congruence is not only ensured by extending quality to all aspects of a service, but also by ensuring consistency within the clientele. A service will usually receive a favourable rating if the customer notes that its other customers are similar to himself. 'Customer portfolio' management is all the more important if customers meet at the point of purchase or consumption, as they do at recreation areas, large scale retail stores, and adult education centers.

Ignoring the congruence factor can have disastrous results. Witness the misguided efforts of the Paris Mass Rapid Transit System. In response to declining passenger numbers, 'Le Metro' launched its famous '*Ticket Chic, Ticket Shock*' advertising campaign. The message it tried to convey: it is chic to ride the subway and the low fares will shock you. After investing heavily in the advertising campaign the company neglected to spruce up the trains and the stations. For a few weeks the campaign seemed destined for success. Passenger numbers did increased. Once commuters realized, however, that the Metro was no more chic than before, they deserted it for good. They figured one 'shock' was enough.

## The concept of quality varies with the culture

It is a common mistake to confuse quality with luxury. A five-star hotel is not the only standard of quality. McDonald's makes quality hamburgers. Quality is a ratio; it is the value obtained in exchange for the price paid. Furthermore, the various components of quality do not have the same weight from one country to another. For example:

- Punctuality. Being ten minutes late in France is not as serious as in Germany; speedy service in an American restaurant is more important than in a British.
- Attention given to the customer. Colorado ski resorts are famous for the attention which they give to skiers; boxes of tissues are available to those awaiting ski lifts, an employee greets you at the entrance to the slopes and another wipes the snow off the seat before you sit down. In Switzerland, a calculator is provided when you are changing money at a teller's window. In Japanese trains, you choose your seat and all seats can be turned to face the running direction of the train.

- The idea of honesty. An American-style handshake agreement does not carry the same weight in France or Italy.

Figure 2.2 shows those dimensions where differences can occur from one country to another. It is in a way a geographical map a traveller can fill in according to his own experiences.

| | Of little importance | | | | | Of great importance | | | | |
|---|---|---|---|---|---|---|---|---|---|---|
| | United Kingdom | United States | France | West Germany | Japan | United Kingdom | United States | France | West Germany | Japan |
| Punctuality | | | | | | | | | | |
| Promptness | | | | | | | | | | |
| Attention | | | | | | | | | | |
| Taking back articles | | | | | | | | | | |
| Personal warmth | | | | | | | | | | |
| Courtesy | | | | | | | | | | |
| Concept of honesty | | | | | | | | | | |
| Quick response | | | | | | | | | | |
| Accurate response | | | | | | | | | | |
| Instructions for use | | | | | | | | | | |
| Respect for the customer | | | | | | | | | | |
| Asking the customer's opinion | | | | | | | | | | |

*Figure 2.2 Primary quality dimensions variables by country*

## Customer satisfaction, a secret to uncover

Many elements influence the perception of quality and complicate an analysis of customer satisfaction. Understanding these influences is especially critical because customers often hide their dissatisfaction with service.

The reason is simple. Most services are received on a one-to-one basis. From the customer's point of view, expressing displeasure can mean incriminating the faulty service giver. The issue becomes very personal and many customers shy away from confrontation. It is much easier to write a complaint letter about a defective transmission than about a clumsy waiter. Yet customer silence is all the more serious for the company when, in terms of service, the customer's displeasure may be very strong. Dissatisfied customers seldom grant the company a second chance. A customer dissatisfied with his first experience is almost always a lost customer.

Experience shows that out of one hundred dissatisfied customers, only four will spontaneously express their discontent. It is essential that a company understands the degree of satisfaction of its customers. Comparing the number of complaint letters to the total number of customers served gives one indication. Setting an acceptable standard for complaints is a subjective process but present opinion suggests that there should be no more than 800 complaint letters for every 100,000 customers served. That is 0.8 per cent. If the complaint ratio rises to the 20 per cent range, an alarm should go off; your customers are extremely unhappy customers!

A complaint ratio under 20 per cent is however no reason for complacency. It may just be an indication that the customers do not know where to address their complaints. Customers may not take the time to inform the offending company of their dissatisfaction, but most will take pleasure in talking about it to friends and relatives. Recent market research revealed that a dissatisfied customer will generally tell eleven people about his misadventure, whereas a satisfied customer will seldom tell more than three people.

## Self-diagnosis

- Who are your customers?
- Can you classify them into homogeneous groups?
- What services do they expect?
- By what criteria do they judge service quality?
- How do these criteria compare with their judgments of five years ago?
- Have they become more demanding?
- Have new criteria appeared?
- Have some changed or ceased to be important at all?
- What is the weakest link in your service delivery chain?
  - in your opinion?
  - in your customers opinions?
- Do you know whether these criteria are different in the countries where you operate?
- To what degree?

# 3

# The Unique Nature of Service Quality

## The difficulty in managing service quality

The quality of a service is more difficult to manage than the quality of a product. A service generally has a greater number of components than does a product, and certainly a lot more visible components. There are many more elements to observe and evaluate about a department store than about an automobile. The customer does not see the bolt that holds the fender in place, but he immediately senses a cashier who has a bad day. It is generally accepted that a customer notices ten service components for every one product component.

Moreover, since customers tend to dwell on the least satisfactory element of a service, high satisfaction rates for services are particularly difficult to achieve. If the error rate is one per cent on ten service criteria, 11 per cent of the customers will be dissatisfied to some degree. (See the explanation of Conditional Statistics below.) If the error rate is five per cent, the proportion of dissatisfied customers goes up to 41 per cent. If a service comprises one hundred quality criteria, an error of one per cent on each of them produces a three per cent customer dissatisfaction rating. The risk of dissatisfaction increases as the number of service quality parameters increases. The more elements there are in a service, the higher the risk of error and the greater the risk of displeasing a customer. Hence, it is simpler to manage service at McDonald's than to manage service in a 3-star restaurant.

The duration of the customer contact also has a direct influence on the risk of error. The longer the transaction takes, the greater the risk one runs of displeasing the customer. It is easier to control quality during a 24-hour hotel stay than during a month-long holiday. (See Figure 3.1.)

CONDITIONAL STATISTICS

Error rates predicated on multiple variables demand special computation. An error in any one component of a service compromises the integrity of the entire service. Thus, it is necessary to compute the possibility of being 'right' at each step of the procedure. The measurement is made by determining the percentage of satisfied customers and multiplying it by an exponent equal to the number of variables. The result is subtracted from 100% to obtain the rate of dissatisfaction.

$$100\% - \left(\frac{\text{satisfied customers}}{100\%\ \text{customers}}\right)^{x} = \text{rate of dissatisfaction}$$

Using data from the examples cited:

$$100\% - \left(\frac{99}{100}\right)^{10} = 11\% \qquad 100\% - \left(\frac{95}{100}\right)^{10} = 41\% \qquad 100\% - \left(\frac{99}{100}\right)^{100} = 63\%$$

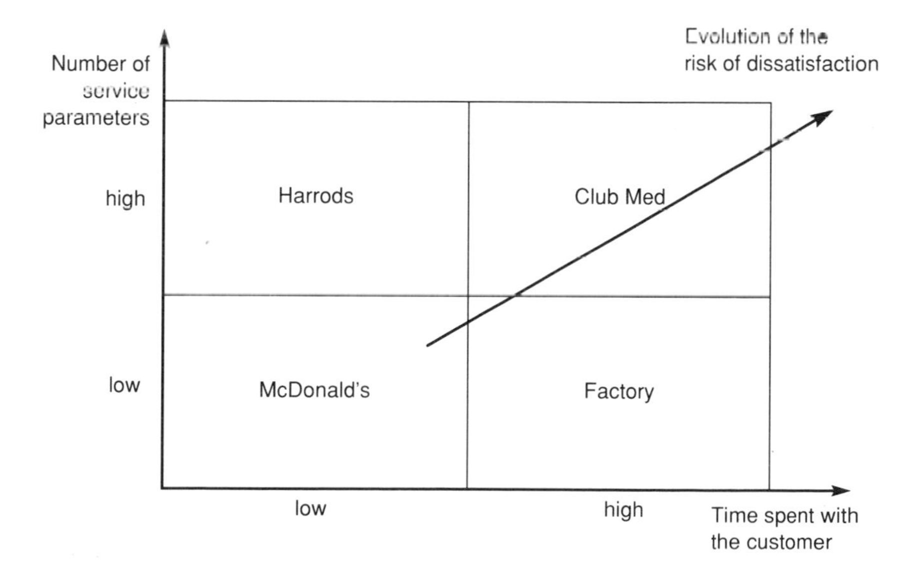


*Figure 3.1 Evolution of the risk of dissatisfaction*

Yet the difficulties do not stop here. Service is temporal. It is often produced and consumed at the same time. A cheerful welcome cannot be produced, checked, stored. This being the case, one cannot 'fix' service quality. Once the error has been committed, its moment is past and cannot be retrieved. The only solution is to try and anticipate errors. When a customer receives an incorrect insurance policy, it is too late to take it back and apologize. When a haircut goes awry, the hairdresser cannot put hair back. When a customer is sick after eating bad oysters, there is only one way to relieve him!

Unlike the product industry, which has developed methods to control product quality, the service industry cannot possibly control quality after 'production'. Sampling, inspection and control do take place, but all by the customer, *at the time of consumption.*

There is no room for rejects. A factory can scrap 20 per cent of its products if they prove to be defective, but it is not possible to scrap 20 per cent of a group of holidaymakers if they are unhappy. The simultaneity of service operations completely modifies the perspective from which quality is managed. In the manufacture of products, error prevention can lead to cost reduction. In providing service, error reduction is a direct guarantee of revenue.

A customer cannot test a service before paying for it. The provider cannot demonstrate the service without actually performing it. Deficient service cannot be resold on the bargain table, nor can it be repaired or exchanged for good service. Hence, the vital importance of doing it right first time. (This subject is covered in Chapter 7.)

Since production and consumption of a service are simultaneous, the person providing a service is not the only one affecting the quality. In service delivery the customer plays a direct and substantial role. Actors often perform better when they feel they are playing to a 'good' audience. The success of a holiday cruise depends, to a large extent, on how well the passengers get on with each other. A computer data service can only provide top performance when utilized by customers who have taken the time to learn how to use it.

In order to manage and control the quality of a service, it is crucial to dissociate those elements of a service which can be effected by the customer from those over which he has no influence. One can control the quality of the latter by handling them as 'industrially' as possible. In a bank, for example, counselling services are effected by officer–customer interactions.

But the same officer usually has responsibility for keeping accurate records of client transactions, balances, etc. The maintenance of these records will not be effected by the client and should be managed in as efficient a manner as possible.

Geographical dispersion also adds to the difficulty of managing service quality. When two factories make a product for the world market, it is easier to control production quality than to control the quality of the hundreds of dealer networks and thousands of selling points which will eventually route the product to the customer.

The broader the area over which a service is dispersed, the greater the risk of deviation from quality standards.

## The cost of quality versus those of non-quality

During the last decade many companies have expended considerable effort to improve the quality of products. Their goal has been to reduce costs and improve profits. By urging people to suggest ways of improving their work methods, managers hoped to reduce inspection time, reworking time, and rejection rates.

Instead of spending money to inspect, rework and/or scrap a rejected product, some companies have invested in quality circles. Ideally, the quality circle will develop ways to improve product quality and find ways to save money.

In the field of services, quality improvement offers little opportunity for cost reduction. On the other hand, the benefits of errorless service are considerable. Positive word-of-mouth publicity always leads to increased sales.

The standards for product and service quality are very different. If a company builds, for instance, one hundred cars and if ten of those are defective and require an extra investment equal to ten per cent of production cost, the total extra cost is one per cent. A 'zero defect' programme will in this case provide a maximum gain of one per cent .

We saw earlier that in the service sector, a satisfied customer passes his enthusiasm onto an average of three others. We also saw that a dissatisfied customer communicates his aggravation to an average of eleven persons. Thus one per cent of dissatisfied customers will generate another 11 per cent of potentially dissatisfied customers.

The head of the Marriott hotel chain talks about 'fifty million moments of truth'. Every day, throughout the world, customers have 50 million contacts with the Marriott chain. The public has 50 million moments to test the company's ability to deliver quality. Each of these moments can create a satisfied or dissatisfied customer. If the customer is satisfied, he will tell three friends. If dissatisfied, he will tell eleven.

Management of service quality often demands considerable investment. Since the service provider must do it right first time, the investment actually buys prevention. But whatever the stakes, the cost of quality is generally less than the cost of non-quality and the yield from service quality can be very high.

First, today's advertising budgets prove that it is more expensive to win a new customer than to strengthen ties to an existing customer.

Next, the manager must compare his investment in prevention to the costs of internal and external deficiency. The box below gives an overview of the components of the cost of total quality. A quality improvement programme recently instituted by a large appliance distribution chain generated from three to five million pounds worth of deficiency cost reduction. The programme itself cost less than ten per cent of the savings generated.

The total cost of quality

- Costs of prevention: expenditures for preventing errors and for 'doing it right first time'.
- Inspection and control costs: expenditures to control quality. Merely performing audits does not accomplish much since the customer has already perceived the problems.
- Costs of internal deficiency: expenditures due to non-quality such as duplicate invoice preparation, reimbursements, sending a letter of apology, plus scrap and rejects (forms, documentation to be redone) for all the tangible parts of the service.
- Costs of external deficiency: the expenditures for convincing new customers to replace lost customers, counteracting negative publicity and recovering the loss of business from customers who do not return.

Even more important is the fact that an investment in service quality is often a source of extra sales. (My experience over nearly a decade shows that every pound invested in service quality produces an average of one hundred pound in sales.) The gains result from a drop in dissatisfaction rate, the positive impact of word-of-mouth publicity (50 to 70 per cent of people choose a service based on word-of-mouth), and the development of stronger ties with existing customers.

The stakes are enormous. Unfortunately, it is often difficult to convince a financial officer of the profitability of investing in quality. Manufacturing has learned to budget scrap reduction, but the service industry has only just begun to recognize its importance.

## Managing service quality involves both people and methods

Industry relies on machines to guarantee product quality. Automation, robotics and computer-assisted manufacturing and design have all played a role. In services, the efforts can only involve people and methods. *Service is a people business.*

A service company can achieve major savings by breaking down its service chain, by standardizing the delivery steps, by simplification and by centralization. The experience of Federal Express is exemplary. After having studied the risks of error during the various phases of routing mail, Federal Express opted to centralize its operations. It built a centre where mail is collected, sorted and redistributed to the various regions of the United States. Federal Express's service is transporting mail quickly and to the right destination. By centralizing all the sorting tasks, the company found a way to minimize errors. Federal Express soon gained a decisive competitive advantage.

Centralization is a method which may be applicable to many other services. Maintenance and repair, for instance, can often be organized from a single centre.

Methodical error prevention also has an effect on the personnel department. A centralized company finds recruitment, hiring, training and communication policies easier to control. It will also find it easier to rally personnel around the idea of quality and commitment.

Thanks to modern data communications networks, financial institutions can now group their services. A major bank has thus developed a system for quickly answering requests for credit. Loan officers dialogue directly with a central file. Naturally, centralization is more valuable when there is a predictability to the customer's requests.

When the service must be 'tailored', decentralization is preferable. A building society's mortgage services, for example, must be assumed by highly qualified staff in local branches.

It is often necessary to break a service down into sub-services, reserving a standard method for the simple and frequent components, and a personalized approach for more specialized applications.

The people/method duo is therefore essential in managing service quality. Neither element can succeed on its own.

My bank manager is an extremely courteous man. Whenever I go to see him I am received most amicably. However, when I enquire after the state of my trust fund the answer invariably is: I will find out for you and let you know within a fortnight. Now consider the following example:

At your service!

During the oil embargo of the 1970s, major oil companies decided to enter the retail business. Exxon, BP, Texaco and others wanted to move product, at the lowest possible cost. (Some even suggested that they also wanted to cut out the middleman.) The 'Self-Service' station was invented. They are now ubiquitous in urban and rural landscapes alike.

The 'service stations' feature well-lit signs which can be seen for miles, and a large number of pumps, each equipped to supply a number of different qualities of petrol.

After the the tank is filled, the customer must leave the car and walk to the cashier's counter. His register is often encased in bullet-proof glass. On the way to the counter the stomach is tempted by a vast array of snacks, beverages and caffeine pills. (For some reason popcorn and fried chicken are always prominently displayed.) There's a rack filled with comic books and magazines, in case the children are getting bored, and a drug shelf with aspirin, car-sickness remedies and cold tablets. Somewhere in the rear of the building one might find a set of toilets. These toilets always come equipped with those disgusting hot air blowers instead of hand towels. (Hand towels must be harder to manage.)

After one's odyssey through the carbohydrate belt, the customer is greeted by an amplified voice (remember the cashier is encased in bullet-proof glass) hawking cigarettes, road maps or oil. Payment is exchanged via a pivoting drawer so that one need never come into direct contact with the cashier.

The system does not work badly if all the customer wants to do is stock up on petrol, sweets and soft drinks.

But driving into this 'service station' with a broken water pump is an entirely different experience. The man hired to help out with refueling problems couldn't find the water pump with a map. (He was hired to fill tanks). The cashier cannot leave his register without setting off a burglar alarm. When asked about a mechanic, he offers that somewhere down the road there used to be one. But he thinks he's in the hospital, or maybe he's out fishing. After all, today is Wednesday. The axiom that service quality has many levels is proven again!

What to do for the broken water pump?

Try feeding it some fried chicken!

## Self-diagnosis

- What is the satisfaction rate of your customers?
- How much does your average customer spend with you in a year?
- How much money did you spend on reimbursements last year?
- How much did you spend on audit, inspection, control? Among your dissatisfied customers, how many will never come back (if you are unable to estimate the figure, take 85 per cent )?
- What are your total sales? What percentage do you stand to lose due to dissatisfied customers? How much would you need to spend to replace the lost customers (in advertising, sales force, promotion)?
- How many customers do you estimate will never come in due to negative word of mouth?
- What is the total cost of your external deficiency?
- How much do you spend on prevention (to prevent service errors)?
- Does your budget procedure permit you to justify increasing expenses to increase customer satisfaction (and the related contribution)?

# 4

# Service Strategies

Monopolies are vanishing. Advertising strategies promoting 'the newest model' and 'the latest fashion' are shortening the life expectancy of goods and services. Technological improvements are making it easier to standardize the delivery of goods and services. Markets are becoming increasingly segmented and customers are increasingly difficult to satisfy. Against this background a company determined to succeed must develop a unique and durable competitive advantage. At present, such an advantage can no longer be ensured without a service strategy. In some areas, a service strategy may be the only way to attract new customers and strengthen the ties to existing ones.

This chapter deals with how a company can design a service strategy by combining its know-how with market expectations. This process begins with questions. Does the firm want to become the Disneyland of recreation? The McDonald's or the Maxim's of food services? The Otis or the Xerox of after-sales service? The Travelodge or the Marriott of the hotel industry? The Swissair or the SAS of the airline industry? Each of these firms has succeeded in defining and implementing a service strategy which satisfies a particular market segment. In each of the cases the service strategy has given the company their unique competitive advantage. Swissair, for example, sells its passengers punctuality and safety, while SAS emphasizes travelling efficiency for the businessman.

## The customer is king

This statement is vital to the development of any effective service strategy! A company cannot exist without customers. In the search of a better 'bottom line' many companies have lost sight of this basic truth.

The illusion that 'it will move off the shelves in any event' has been refuted in most businesses. The 'old days' will never come back.

Companies which have accepted the central importance of the customer will achieve exceptional results, even while functioning in depressed markets. In the furniture industry, the Ikea furniture-warehouses have won increased market shares in the last few years. It is quite an experience to visit their stores where the entire shopping experience is organized with the customer in mind, i.e., clear and comprehensible catalogues and order forms, plenty of car parking space and trolleys, easy access, delivery or take-it-home-yourself options, a play room for the children and even a comfortable snack area where the customer can rest weary feet.

In another depressed sector, the garment industry, Benetton has developed a competitive edge. In twenty years, it has established four thousand selling points throughout the world. The outlets are kept small to give the customer the feeling of shopping in a boutique.

The customer must be the starting point of every service strategy. The objective of a good service strategy *must* be to hold on to existing customers while winning over new ones. It is vital to understand customer needs and to address them. Companies which ignore this elementary principle will not stay in business for very long.

Contrary to the ideas of certain business leaders, today's customer is no longer willing to adapt to inconvenient company policies. The company has to adapt to customer needs. It is a good idea to consider investing at least one pound to address customer needs for every pound invested in advertising. If one is not willing to accept this fact, the advertising budget might best be paid directly to the shareholders.

There are two ways to capture a market sector: wage a price war or offer a unique and superior difference.

## Competitive price or competitive difference?

As a general rule, most European companies are ill-equipped to win price wars. Winning would mean reducing costs. In the cost-price spiral, there is always a competitor who thinks he can do better. That competitor may have access to cheap labour or, in the case of American or Japanese firms whose domestic markets are quite large, he may be able to benefit from the experience curve (lower prices to capture a market share which will subsequently lead to lower production costs).

Price alone rarely provides a long-term competitive advantage. Even if a company succeeds in developing a radically new technology to reduce cost, imitators will not lag far behind. On the other hand, European firms do have the know-how which gives them an advantage in a competition based on 'difference'. Restaurants and catering, gastronomy, perfume, fashion, tourism, recreation and resorts, and software design are all fields where French companies have been able to capture major positions in world markets. The United Kingdom, on the other hand, enjoys an excellent know-how in the fields of financial services and retailing

Among the tactics of differentiation, service orientation can provide a winning edge. Even banks are being forced to adopt a service orientation. Smaller, less cumbersome businesses are offering services formerly the exclusive domain of banks. Squeezed between dynamic competitors, such as building societies and the Trustee Saving Bank, and the astronomical costs of cash routing, (due to superfluous branches and earlier transaction-due dates) banks are rediscovering their customers who, in the meantime, have evolved a different perception of their needs for financial services.

Contrary to an idea which is still widespread in the banking world, the customer is no longer apathetic. A recent study demonstrated that 25 per cent of customers switch banks in any five year period. Their decision is motivated by displeasure with services. Furthermore, people are spreading their business more and more among several financial institutions. 'Old-style' banks could take a real beating. To prove this point one only has to look at the fact that banks are beginning to hear from customers objecting to excessive charges on current accounts. It is a self-defeating strategy. The customer is being asked to subsidize the bank's inefficiencies, but gets nothing in return. That is why more and more people are switching banks. They are tired of long queues in front of the service tills; annoyed with statements that arrive at mid-month with ever-increasing overdraft charges, and frustrated at not knowing to whom they can express their displeasure.

A service-based battle means:

- In a product business: a battle over everything which the customer has the right to expect of the company in addition to the basic product . . . service before, during and after the sale.
- In a service business: a battle for everything which concerns the service features and the experience(s) involved.

Examples of good service orientation:

- The sale of a computer is preceded by a needs analysis, accompanied by user-friendly documentation, by assistance at installation and start-up, and followed by fast and effective trouble-shooting and repair.
- The sale of kitchen utensils in a department store is preceded by convenient parking, easy and pleasant access to the store, accompanied by knowledgeable sales personnel, wide selection, and culminates with efficient check-out, appropriate packaging and acceptance of credit cards.
- A hotel offers a restaurant, a bar, a trained service staff, business services including at least a photo copier and a fax machine, currency exchange, an exercise facility and perhaps even an automobile rental office.
- A service-oriented haircut is not simply shortening the customer's hair, but also fast if designed for busy people; in the latest style, if aimed at the style conscious; complemented by a cup of coffee, if designed to meet a need for pleasure and relaxation.
- Financial trust service should include a warm and confidential welcome, skill in analysing the customer's needs and answering questions, unambiguous documentation concerning fees and performance, instantaneous information about the value of the portfolio, anticipation of future trends, and guaranteed follow-up.

An effective service orientation will identify the needs and expectations of a target clientele beyond the obvious qualities of the product or basic service. It should complete and reinforce the company's basic marketing strategy. In the future, every company will have to depend on a service orientation to attract and retain customers.

## Product service strategies

Keeping the dimensions of price and service in mind, a product supplier has three strategic options, which are also illustrated in Figure 4.1: *high fashion* (very special high priced service), *custom-made* (personalized service at reasonable price) and *ready-to-wear* (minimum service and low price).

The three strategies often co-exist in the same market sector, but each is aimed at a different market segment. The 'high fashion' strategy targets the customer for whom price has little importance, but who demands a 'high touch' level of service.

The 'ready-to-wear' strategy targets the customer who cares more about price than service. The 'custom-made' strategy on the other hand attempts to satisfy the customer who is sensitive to *good quality* service for a *reasonable price*.

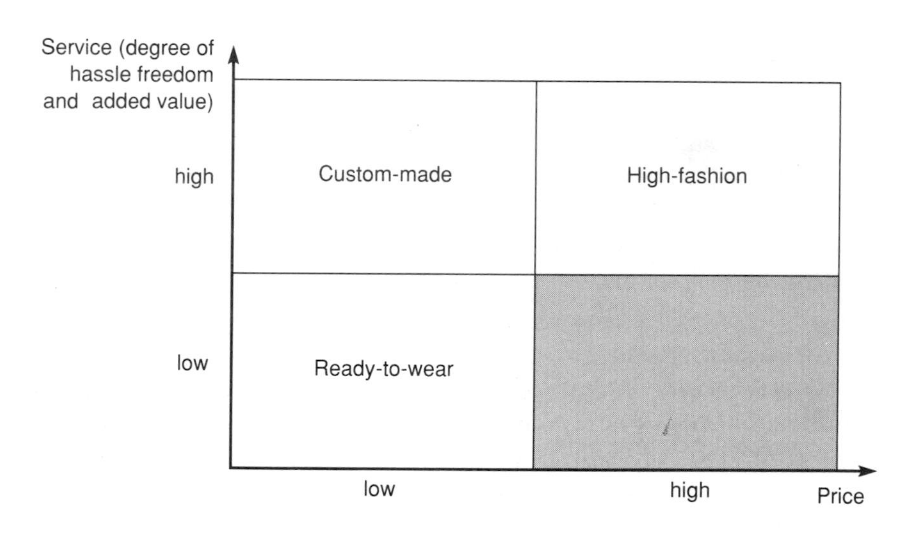


*Figure 4.1 The product service strategies*

The three strategies can also fit within the product range of the same manufacturer. This is particularly noticeable in the automobile industry where each major manufacturer has a model to appeal to every bank balance and every life style.

Certain products do not lend themselves to a service policy. That does not mean, however, that creative management cannot devise one. Whether selling chemicals, electronic components, timber or canned goods, an effective service policy can provide an edge. The British turkey producer, Bernard Mathews, found an edge. So did Crown Cork & Seal, the small aerosol and food can manufacturer. Starting with a slim five per cent market share and facing competitors as powerful as Continental Can, Crown Cork & Seal now performs two or three times better in terms of margin and return on invested capital. How? By conducting a 'high fashion' policy with substantial added value. This company:

- concentrates on applications where the container influences the quality of the content (pharmaceutical products);
- works in close coordination with the research people from client firms in order to reduce the costs of using containers and packing;
- provides customers with specialized machinery for filling and closing particular containers;
- locates small factories near customers to ensure fast delivery and even opens factories throughout the world to follow its customers abroad;
- reserves extra production capacity to respond to customer's last-minute needs; and
- conducts surveys in supermarkets to pin-point customer preferences.

It uses this data to propose better packaging ideas. Its customers are ecstatic.
Who pays for the added value? Not the customer. Alongside its service policy, Crown Cork & Seal rigorously controls its overheads and invests in the latest technologies to continually improve its productivity. Machines are often replaced, even before they are fully depreciated, so that the company can maintain its competitive advantages: speed, flexibility and research.

A service strategy can also be implemented by orienting one's efforts toward being hassle-free. Every manufacturer is interested in reducing costs due to machine failure, maintenance and downtime? To an oil drilling crew a 'same day' repair policy would be priceless.

Many elements can be included in a product service policy. The customer can be aided in logistics, training, method changes, inventory accounting to minimize the costs of restocking or stockout, and even in nature of the manufacturing process itself. Reaching zero hassle is a priceless goal. Alas, it is rarely achieved.

## Service strategy and product life cycle

The best service strategy will change according to the product's stage of development because customer expectations also evolve with the product.

Service is less important for an innovation. The innovator may be a 'sole source'. Concerned with the benefits offered by the innovation, the customer will excuse service shortcomings. Since there is no equivalent product he has to take what he can get. For his part, the innovator generally prefers to invest in the development of the product itself. However, the customer may have a poor understanding of the product and so perceive a risk in adopting it. For a service with a high added value, for instance providing start-up assistance, shared analysis of needs and applications and follow-up, is therefore appropriate. This will mean providing a service system.

During the growth phase, competition intensifies. To maintain the Number 1 position, the innovator must now provide more and better service. A competitor may soon offer a similar product at a lower price. At this point the service must not only provide added value. It must also be more hassle-free.

In the mature phase, the market may be saturated. Three different options must be considered:

- a ready-to-wear strategy: minimum service for a low price,
- a high fashion strategy: extensive service for a market which asks for it and is ready to pay the price,
- an open range strategy: a choice of various levels of service.

| Product development phase / Service strategies | Launching | Growth | Maturity | Decline |
|---|---|---|---|---|
| Dominant dimension of service | Added value | Being hassle-free | Added value and being hassle-free | High added value or withdrawal |
| Strategic options | High fashion | Custom-made | Ready-to-wear or custom-made | High fashion or withdrawal |

*Figure 4.2 Service strategies and product life cycle*

The last option has the advantage of serving customers with different needs; offering little service to the experienced customer who prefers to pay less while pampering the neophyte who needs extensive assistance.

Depressed industries may be limited to a few 'high fashion' target markets. Such a condition forces the most difficult decision: fight it out on a price basis, or withdraw from the market. See Figure 4.2.

### *Service strategies and customer value chain*

A service strategy can only succeed if the company coordinates all of the elements in the customer value chain. This chain might include any number of raw material suppliers, component manufacturers, middlemen and dealers and finally, the customer. For example, to help a customer understand the applications for a product, it may be necessary to understand the materials which are incorporated into it at manufacture.

Serving the customer may require training dealers. Mistral, the sailboard manufacturer, continues to dominate the sailboard market by training its dealers, by making it mandatory for them to stock spare parts as well as finished products, by organizing the second-hand market for them, and by creating sailboard schools.

## Service strategies for services

The relationship between price and service also exists in the service sector. However, the 'hassle free' and 'added value' dimensions are replaced by the 'basic service features' and the 'experience'. In the service sector there are also three strategic options: the *gastronomy* option: high price and service; the *formula* option: custom-made service at a reasonable price; and the *fast-food* option: minimum service at a moderate price. (See Figure 4.3.)

In the service sector the level of basic service is determined by two elements: the *intensity* of the interaction between the supplier and the customer, and the *duration* of that contact. The 'gastronomy' option targets customers who seek highly personalized service, i.e., a great deal of interaction and long contact. Alternatively, the 'fast food' strategy seeks to satisfy the customer who is price conscious. This customer buys service with minimal interaction and a short contact period. Figure 4.4 positions four types of customer treatment where the service is very different in terms of intensity and duration of contact.

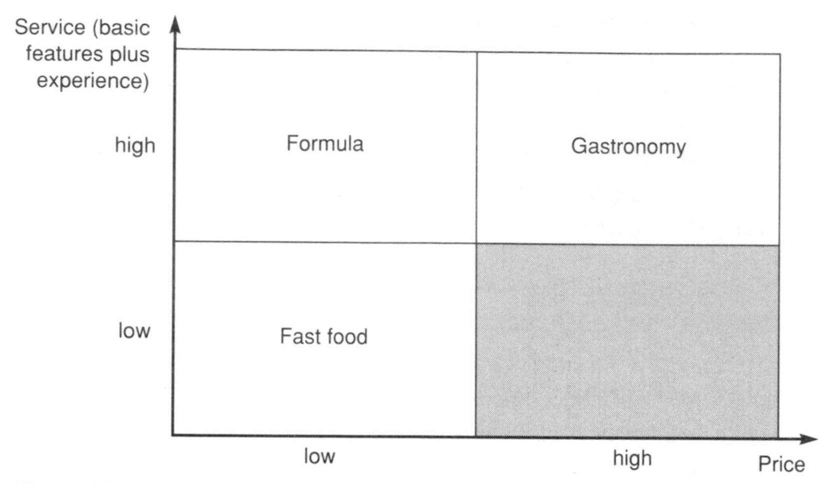

*Figure 4.3 The service strategies for services*

The more the service supplier wishes to intensify the interaction with the customer, the more he must personalize the service. On the other hand, if he wishes to reduce the cost of the features, he must seek ways to increase standardization.

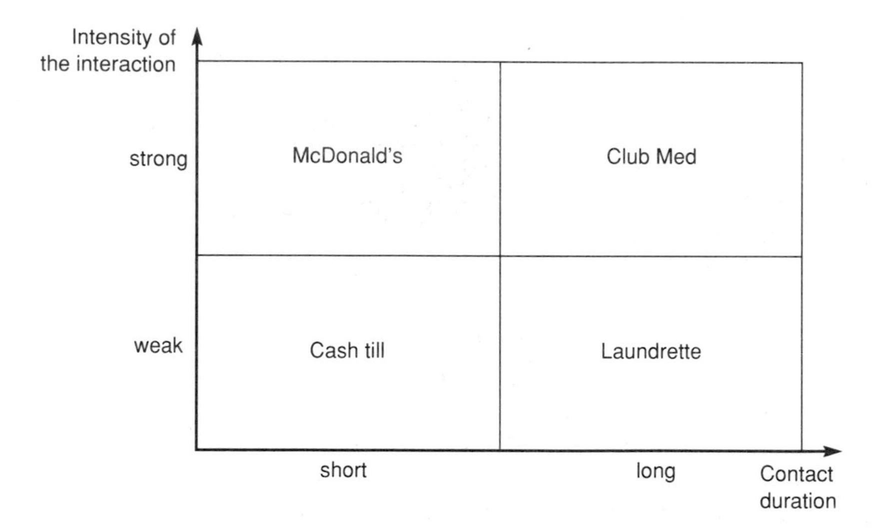


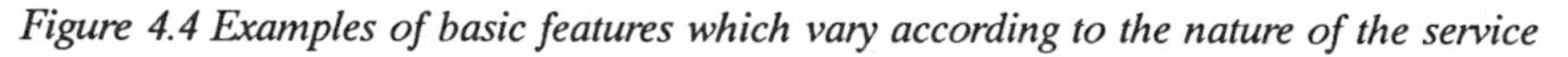
*Figure 4.4 Examples of basic features which vary according to the nature of the service*

Therefore, the choice of a *basic* service strategy must be based on the possibility of personalizing or standardizing individual features. These two factors will give the features high or low service density (see Figure 4.5).

Most types of basic service features can be covered by different strategic options. As with industrial products, the different strategies can co-exist within a service sector as long as they create unique and durable competitive advantages. The variety of restaurants listed in the *Yellow Pages* proves the point. It is more difficult to imagine a similar diversity in health services or management consultancy. Health services have traditionally been delivered according to a 'gastronomy' policy, with costly and highly personalized service (strong interaction between the doctor and his patient, long contact duration). The recent proliferation of emergency, 24-hour, health-care centres indicates, however, that even the medical profession is open to innovation.

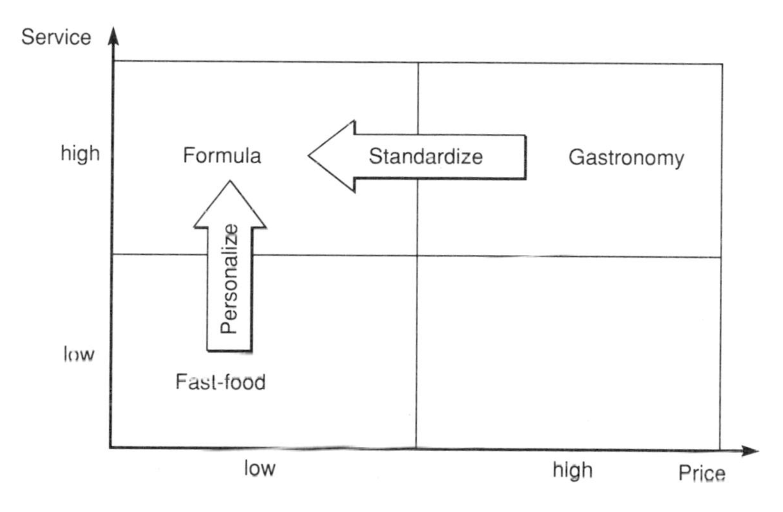


*Figure 4.5 Strategic options for services*

In the UK, day clinics have even started to offer automated health diagnosis and will perform vasectomies without hospitalization.

## The 'gastronomy' strategy

The 'gastronomy' strategy is the most personal; it lavishes attention on the customer and serves him over a longer period of time. It assumes high costs and therefore generally targets a limited market. This does not mean that the company which opts for this strategy will not try to reduce costs and increase productivity. On the contrary!

The wager of a gastronomy policy is that the company can maintain the high level of personalization. *Conforming to the level of excellence* is the key factor in the success of such an approach.

Many believe that the gastronomy strategy can only apply to luxury items. This is not necessarily the case. A printer can just as well offer up-scale service. So can a dry cleaner or a building caretaker.

## The 'formula' strategy

The 'formula' strategy is the most ambiguous one. It is often more difficult to implement than the 'gastronomy' or 'fast-food' strategies. It involves targeting a market which is larger than the 'happy few' of gastronomy, while still offering personalized service. Prices will be established to appeal to the widest number of people. Here, the wager is to conceive methods which are less expensive (lower contact cost), but which still personalize service. There are some interesting examples:

### *The club*

The club idea is still new in European management circles. The customer becomes a 'member' of a group and as such he benefits from various advantages. Since the group members generally share common interest, marketing is done by word-of-mouth and promotional costs are minimized. Club services (newsletter, special offers, etc. . .) personalize the service while at the same time, standardizing it. The club formula is very promising but it has its pitfalls. Too much success can be dangerous. If the club gets too large, it becomes impersonal and the 'club aspect', with all its benefits, can be lost.

An increasing number of service companies are, however, using the club idea; automobile rental agencies, airlines, and mail order financial services head the list. Holiday Inn, for instance, offers special services to members of their club, including special rates and improved in-room facilities.

### *Information*

Many companies are succeeding in reducing capital cost without adversely affecting service quality by employing sophisticated new methods of information and communication. Benetton, for example, never leases retail spaces with more than six hundred square feet. All the merchandise is on display. The company avoids paying premium prices for on-site storage space, but can, thanks to a very sophisticated telecommunications system, still respond instantaneously to customer demand.

*Standardization of know-how*

This approach, which consists of developing a specific body of knowledge, then detailing and standardizing the analysis and communication methods, is particularly well-known among consultancy firms and its advantages are numerous. The consultancy firm so amasses a unique body of knowledge which distinguishes it from the competition.

It furthermore has now an excellent means of controlling quality and conformance with a desired level of excellence. Standardization also facilitates the training of newcomers and so provides cost-efficiency, because if every employee works in a standardized system one can often make better use of junior, less expensive personnel working next to a senior, more experienced member of staff. This is called a pyramid of skills.

Standardization of methods, training, and communication, can be applied to many business sectors. A travel agency might develop an approach which would allow new employees to handle simple questions and a more experienced staff to do the travel counselling. Once the method is defined, judgment calls are minimized. So is the possibility of inconsistency. That will translate into increased profits.

*Increase customer participation in providing the service*

Another way of reducing costs while keeping up the level of personalization is to train the customer to play a more active role in the service. Telephone companies educate their customers to choose certain time periods. Many restaurant chains opt for salad bars where the customers are invited to help themselves. Hotels place shoe-shine machines next to the coffee machines, to the great satisfaction of the guests. Computer manufacturers train their customers to manage spare parts inventories and to perform in-house maintenance. However, caution is needed. The border between the 'formula' and the 'fast-food' options can get blurred. The more the customer is led to intervene, the less personalized the service becomes and the greater the risk of losing the customer. There is no substitute for a good understanding of customer needs and expectations.

## The 'fast-food' strategy

By maximizing standardization and minimizing contact duration, the 'fast-food' service supplier reduces costs, and therefore prices. He appeals to a market which is more concerned with price than with the level of service. Kitchens in institutional restaurants, for example, are shrinking. Precooked dishes, reheated in microwave ovens are replacing the enormous kitchens where armies of chefs once tended hot stoves.

Mail-order firms offer catalogues which seriously rival shop windows (some of which do not even dare to display their prices). And each of us has another new friend, the automatic teller.

## Service strategy: a promise

A service strategy is always based on a promise made to the customer. McDonald's promises quality, speed and cleanliness; Club Med, happiness; Marks and Spencers, the best quality at the most reasonable price; Travelodge, easy access at a bargain price.

The firm which chooses to compete on a service front must design a promise based upon the needs of a target clientele, communicate it clearly, and above all, be faithful to it.

If the promise can be expressed in less than one hundred words, it is a good sign. It is a good indication that the company is service oriented. If it can be stated in less than fifty words, the company has every chance of becoming the leader in its field. If the promise fits into twenty five words, the company cannot help but make a fortune.

The formulation of the promise is the responsibility of top-level management. The promise formulated by top management will provided the basis upon which middle managers will define specific service standards.

### The Swissair Promise

The customer will always:

- be transported in the most modern aircraft,
- in the safest possible manner,
- receive traditional Swiss hospitality,
- receive a dynamic response to customer needs
- receive the assistance in the coordination of his travel needs, even when the arrangements demand the service of outside providers.

Swissair does not promise the most modern fleet, merely a modern fleet. Singapore Airlines replaces its aircraft every two years and assures it in their promise. Swissair does not say 'anticipate the needs', but 'a dynamic response to needs'. Incidentally, Swissair was the last European airline to introduce the business class.

**The Club Med promise**

The customer will always:

- be housed in a facility that is attractive, clean, where everything works;
- be served with attentiveness, generosity and imagination;
- eat and drink according to personal taste (all you want, when you want);
- make new friends easily and learn something new;
- have no worry and run no danger;
- enjoy the village from the moment of arrival.

**The promise of Langan's Brasserie**

- this is not a crossroads, it is a meeting place;
- this is not only ambience, it is entertainment;
- see and be seen;
- one does not simply eat, one spends an evening;
- one does not simply come in, one makes an entrance.

The first purpose of a promise is to facilitate internal communication. Every employee must understand the strategy in terms of customer benefits. If the objective is universally understood, it will be easier to achieve.

Only after management is secure in the knowledge that all employees understand the promise, should this promise be offered to the customer. An unkept promise is worse than no promise at all. At the very least the company must commit itself to keeping it; to providing guarantees which fulfil the commitment or indemnify an unkept promise.

Finally, there can be only one promise for each target clientele. Each customer has his own needs and expectations, and a promise, no matter how well formulated and kept, will not succeed if it is addressed to customers who do not want or need it. Keeping the promise must be a company-wide effort to which the entire organization must dedicate itself, from procedures to people, from finance to communications. A company may have as many distinct organizations as it has promises. Banks, traditionally organized by product, are re-orienting themselves by market and, within each market (institutions, companies, individuals) by market segment.

IBM, which receives 50 per cent of its sales from services, understands the premise very well. It recently instituted a reorganization by industry.

At the last Paris data processing show, a young French software firm 'promised' a software program capable of transcribing handwritten text into a word processor language. Thinking about my manuscript and my terrible handwriting, I was quick to ask: 'How much does it cost? I would like to have one; when can I have one?'

Nobody could answer me. I hope, for the firm's sake, that it will deign to sell its product before people have to drop to their knees begging. I would not be surprised if, one day, the invention wins the annual French invention prize. However, given the lack of a service strategy, I, like many others, will probably buy the American or Japanese brand.

## Self-diagnosis

- What are your various market segments?
- What does each of them want?
- What strategy have you chosen to service them? 'Gastronomy', 'Formula', or 'Fast-Food'?
- Have you defined promises to your customer?
- How is each promise expressed?
- Does the promise match what the customers want?
- Is it written in terms of results for the customer? Does it make you unique? Different from your competitors?
- Does it contain less than one hundred words?

# 5

# Communicating the Service

Communication plays a central role in the success of a service strategy. It is indispensable for broadening the client base, increasing fidelity, motivating personnel and giving them a precise understanding of the chosen quality standards.

Communication must be accurately targeted. It loses all effectiveness when it tries to be everything for everyone. Finally, communication is not limited to an advertising message or technical documentation. It covers all direct and indirect circumstances which bring the customer into contact with the company.

## Emphasize the difference

Communication is the only way to declare your 'difference', your edge over the competition. Effective communication sends a message to the customer, associating product and service, basic features and service experience. Singapore Airlines' advertisements always feature young, smiling Singaporean women. The customer is supposed to associate Asiatic graciousness and hospitality with the airline.

The communication itself can be a means of differentiation. When Lufthansa states that it is a German company, this is not meant as a truism. It emphasizes its expertise in terms of organization, punctuality and efficiency. At Lufthansa, service means anticipating problems. The advertisement picturing two technicians in front of an aircraft and captioned: 'At Lufthansa, the service begins long before your first cocktail', says it well.

Finally, communication is a powerful tool for managing the expectations of a target clientele. When Scotrail launched a campaign to convince passengers that the train was not quite such a bad idea after all, passenger numbers increased significantly without actual adaptation of the rolling stock, and the image of British Rail improved drastically in Scotland.

## Mould the customer's expectations

Most customers have a preconceived notion about service quality. Favourable or unfavourable prejudices can be influenced by communication. In one famous restaurant, the top of the menu announces: 'Cooking is an art and art is composed of patience'. Result? The impatient customer is no longer in a hurry.

There is a natural temptation to downgrade the customer's expectations, so as to pleasantly surprise him when the service is rendered. This is a mistake. On the other hand, it can be just as harmful to inflate expectations.

### Promise less

If the promise communicated is inferior to the service, one runs the risk of missing the appropriate customer and attracting an unsuitable one, who finds the lower service promise attractive. Promising a 'speedy repair', communicates a lesser service than promising 'repair within 24 hours'. The less sophisticated customer may be pleasantly surprised, but knowledgeable customers will buy from the competitor who promises a shorter and more specific repair time.

### Promise more

A promise which inflates the customer's expectations gives rise to potential disappointment and can result in terminal desertion. Singapore Airlines makes certain that only female flight attendants serve passengers. After all, it promises attractive, Asian hospitality. The hairy-armed stewards work in the galley, unseen by the passengers.

## Reduce the customer's risk perception

The risk involved in using a service is always a major concern. It is not enough to reduce the risk by compiling a wide range of accompanying services. It may be necessary to address the customer's fears.

Word of mouth and a company's reputation can be important to the hesitant customer. A company's purpose-designed communication can also have an influence on the customer's perception of the risk. The message may cover the customers fears directly. It may be more subtle, quote references and describe successful experiences. Another approach is to strengthen the firm's public profile. This option reassures potential and existing customers of the permanence of the firm.

American Express has founded its entire communication campaign on personal testimonies by celebrities.

## Making the service tangible

If product-oriented communication must address intangible attributes, the opposite is true for a service.

Whether it be an car or a household appliance, a consumer product is seldom purchased exclusively for its technical performance. A product can also provide prestige, fulfil a dream or create some other psychological advantage which only communication can convey.

Cadbury's Flake is not just a chocolate bar, it has sexual connotations; Heineken is not just a lager, but a magical potion that makes the impossible happen.

Services are generally intangible. Their 'messages' must communicate advantages through tangible means. If the customer seeks the exotic, he may be satisfied by a photo of palm trees along a white sandy beach. If the promise includes opulence at a moderate price, a photo of sumptuous buffets may address his wants.

Visual communication takes on a special importance for services; it comprises the tangible evidence of the promise. But it must be credible, coherent and followed up by a service which fulfils the promise.

## Where service is involved, everything is communication

What good is a glossy, full-colour newspaper advertisement if the customer is greeted in shabby surroundings? Keeping a service promise can be very difficult. It demands constant effort and mobilization of all the resources of the company. One weak link in the chain will disappoint the customer and the entire chain will take the blame.

Every aspect of a service company should contribute toward communicating the company's unique position. Advertising is only part of the package. The graciousness of the receptionist, the telephone answering service, the speed of access to the relevant person, the handling of complaint letters, the decor of the premises, as well as the appearance of the company vehicles, the manners of the personnel, will all play important roles. In the field of service, everything is communication.

The Elis-Europe company rents linens. Its trucks are always brand new and meticulously polished. The customer concludes that the same can be said about Elis' linens. A renowned Paris bakery delivers its pastries in a van which looks like a huge, pink gift box. An excellent signal!

British Rail has implemented a service improvement campaign which involved sending their employees on a training course known as the BR 'Charm School'. They wanted to tell their customers how much friendlier and helpful their staff were, so they mounted a major television advertising campaign. The only trouble was that only a relatively small percentage of their employees had been on the course when the campaign started. The credibility of the advertising campaign was therefore immediately lost.

Not long ago, a French insurance group adopted the slogan: 'Being Number 1 gives us special responsibilities'. Shortly thereafter the company put one of its rental buildings on the market, giving its tenants the option to buy their apartments. Many tenants wrote to ask for additional information. Their inquiries were never answered. Two months later tenants received letters notifying them that their options have expired. It apparently never occurred to the company that tenants might also need insurance.

## Service by telephone: a powerful way to strengthen or weaken a company's level of excellence

Many companies do business exclusively over the telephone. To most others, the telephone is an indispensable resource. The image of a company and its services is communicated in the most literal sense, in each of its hundreds of daily phone calls. To ensure the level of excellence that the company has promised to provide, the following fundamental questions must be answered:

- Who answers the telephone? How? How quickly? In what tone of voice?
- Are calls efficiently routed? Is there an answering machine or answering service after hours?
- How are complex questions handled? Are customers annoyed at the choice of 'hold music'?

Telephone service must be managed with the same care as manufacturing or accounting. First, a list of the parameters which come into play from the moment the receiver is lifted must be prepared. For each of the parameters, a quality standard must then be specified. The quality of the service for each parameter will be measured by the standard. The manager can compile data tracking: the number of lost calls, the average number of rings before answering, the average time the customer must wait before getting an answer or reaching the appropriate extension, and the number of written or verbal complaints about the professionalism of the person(s) answering the phone.

A 'telephone smile' is not enough. The company's telephone system should be constantly monitored to make certain incoming lines are sufficient to handle volume, that the while-you-were-out message system works efficiently and that inquiries are answered in a timely fashion. Remember: an exasperated customer can easily become someone else's customer.

## The welcome: an encounter which goes beyond the reception desk.

It is often and wrongfully supposed that a welcome policy consists of placing an attractive receptionist alongside an immense bouquet of flowers. A welcome takes place every time the company comes into contact with the customer, in- or outside of its facility. The welcome can have many variables: a visit to the customer's home or a business appointment, at the company headquarters or at a dealership.

Here again, a smile is not the only parameter. Calling the customer by name, dressing according to the nature of the service and punctuality are all factors which raise the welcome's level of service excellence.

A good bartender will be aware of every customer entering the bar, even when he is busy. A slight nod will then tell the customer that he is noticed and welcome. A receptionist can 'send' a similar recognition signal to an incoming customer, even while she is on the telephone. Without going as far as to actually say 'Good Morning' to each incoming customer (as happens on every floor of a Japanese department store), it would be helpful to train reception personnel to interrupt their conversation when a customer arrives, without giving him the impression that he is the interruption.

### Documentation, the pauper of communication in services

It is striking to note that service companies generally give their documentation an importance which is inversely proportional to the importance given by manufacturers to their products.

Bankers, car rental firms, restaurants and consultants should regularly review their documentation to make certain that it remains consistent with their service promise. Retailers should pay similar attention to catalogues, invoices, and letterhead. *All* documentation should reflect the level of excellence stated in the promise. I dedicate the following example to the sceptics among us.

> A pension fund provider once sent all its potential customers, just before they bought a pension, a gorgeous brochure, full of promises. Once these potential customers had become actual customers, all they received were anonymous photocopies demanding instant responses. A magnificent example of inexcusable communication!

## Dependence on dealers

The problem of communication is more complicated when the company does not have direct contact with its customer. Such companies must make certain that the dealer's communication with the customers conforms to the desired level of excellence. This may be difficult because the dealers, who are not always exclusive, may have their own priorities and opinions.

One of the ways to make the communications conform, is to negotiate joint actions with the dealers.

This collaboration naturally depends upon the relative strengths of the parties. The better the company is known to the final customer, the easier it will be to convince dealers to cooperate. It is particularly important to make the dealers understand the company's quality standards and convince them that it is in their own interest to ensure perfect homogeneity with the service promised.

To ensure a continuity of image in the United States, Club Med convinced travel agencies to allocate part of their commission to joint ventures. The Club built an administrative training centre where it has sponsored training programmes, conducted advertising conception and direct-marketing campaigns, all with agency in-put and cooperation. It found a way to standardize documentation.

Participating travel agencies sacrifice part of their commission in exchange for increased sales. The process works at both ends. The company protects the coherence of its communication policy.

This chapter discussed the value of communications and their potential influence on customer expectations. It is true that internal communications are equally important to the development of a sound service strategy. Internal communications are discussed in the next chapter.

## Self-diagnosis

- What is your target market?
- Do you tend to inflate your promise or to deflate it?
- What are the real relationships between your service and what you communicate to your customer?
- Is the intangible made tangible? How?
- Your telephone answering, your welcome and reception, your sales and non sales documentation, your offices, vehicles, your answers to complaint letters, the skills and manners of your dealers, do they measure up to your advertising? Do they make your service more tangible or do they leave many questions unanswered?

# 6

# Service Quality Standards

Unlike the product industry, which measures performance in units, watts, joules, inches or pounds, the service industry has not yet developed a standardization for the measurement of service standards. Some industries create operating standards which are of little or no interest to the customer. Hotels, for example, may have standards for setting a table, waiting on tables, or making a bed. These data relate more closely to a Taylorist tradition than to quality management.

It is critical to develop service quality standards in order to verify performance and to determine whether a promise is kept. In order to be operational, quality standards must be:

- expressed from the customer's point of view,
- measurable,
- used from the top to the bottom of the organization.

## A standard is set on the basis of customer expectations

In order to become a true performance indicator and not simply an operational rule, a standard must be defined in terms of results for the customer, i.e., the customer expects . . ., the customer wants . . ., the customer shall have . . . .

Then the tasks which must be performed to satisfy the customer will have to be identified, i.e., reception personnel must . . ., the hostess will . . ., the repairman will . . . .

Once these tasks are fully specified, and only then, can the manager develop methods for accomplishing the tasks.

RESULT EXPECTED BY THE CUSTOMER

→ TASKS TO BE PERFORMED

→ OPERATING METHODS

A service quality standard must be based on customer needs. It is the only way to guarantee conformity. Every employee should know 'what to do', 'how to do it' and particularly, 'why it is important'.

Hotel guests generally appreciate a personalized welcome. Marriott hotel bellmen have been instructed to involve guests in conversation whenever possible. They are instructed to take special note of departure stickers on the customer's luggage. This information provides an instant entree to conversation.

A number of women's magazines send new subscribers a leaflet entitled: 'Everything you need to know to enjoy your subscription'. It described a number of service quality standards concerning the mailing label, address changes, subscription/invoicing procedures and options concerning sale of subscriber lists. The codes used on the mailing label are explained so the reader can see at a glance when his subscription is due for renewal. The subscriber is promised that an address change will take less than four weeks, and that the process will taken even less time if he phones in the relevant information. The magazine is guaranteed to arrive no later than four days after publication. A simple post card will ensure that the subscriber is removed from mailing lists, which are regularly sold to a variety of marketing services. The leaflet also tells the subscriber whom to address or telephone, at what times and what days.

A standard defines the tasks designed to satisfy the customer. Nothing prevents a business from doing more. Elvia, the French insurance and travel assistance company, illustrates this well. It sends flowers and a get well card to policy holders which it has returned to France due to illness or accident, even though the holiday insurance policy cost as little as ten pounds!

It is astonishing that estate agencies, which collect huge commissions from residential sales, do not make similar efforts to thank new home buyers.

## A standard must be measurable

Conviviality, graciousness and friendliness are difficult to measure by quantitative standards. Quantification is, however, not always necessary. It is far more important to know whether or not a quality actually exists. A smile is not measured by its length but by its presence. A measurement can be seen as a ratio or a continuum.

Nevertheless, one must try to break down service behaviour into quantifiable elements. The speed of a function should be measurable in hours, minutes or seconds. Courtesy is a more difficult matter. Did the customer receive a 'Good Morning' or not? Was he asked how he was doing? In some services, the welcome is the main cause of customer satisfaction or dissatisfaction, and this warrants the attempts to improve our understanding and definition of the subject. Mr Goirand of the Westminster Hotel offers the following wisdom:

> 'To welcome someone, is to recognize him and to give him hospitality. The guest has travelled. He has come from far away. We need to simultaneously calm him and show him that he has come to the right place'.

Recognition and hospitality are two elements which are measurable. They consist of a number of identifiable components:

- a smile, showing a sign of pleasure at seeing someone;
- verbal communication, greeting the person, knowing his name, speaking to him about his home town;
- communicating with gestures: all the signs which signify recognition of the guest and which confirm his welcome (avoid turning your back to him or blocking his way, for example);
- visual communication: all the physical elements which enhance the guest's feeling of security and well-being, such as direction signs;
- written communication: e.g., the hotel registration card, the travel agency brochure, the furniture dealer's catalogue or the policy issued by an insurance company, brochures and folders, each document in the guest's language, easy to read and understand;
- the competence of the person providing the welcome: their ability to answer the guest's or customer's questions and solve any problems that may arise;
- tangibility of the welcome: a warm and comfortable welcome, appropriate to the service supplied (it would be unnatural to seat a McDonald's customer in a leather armchair, just as it would be incongruous not to install a telephone in the guest room of a five star hotel);
- continuity of welcome: reception is not limited to a first contact, everything must continue to welcome, from check-in to sales, from the invoicing service to the repair service.

When a welcome is broken down into its various elements, it becomes obvious that it is more than a question of properly greeting someone. Some people will do it better than others. A welcome is something which can be learned. But, first, it may need to be taught.

Sometimes a welcome involves no human contact. This type should be easier to control!

> Have you ever tried finding a small town in a part of the country you do not really know? Your destination, Sticksbridge, is listed on the exit sign on the motorway and it is even signposted at the end of the sliproad.
>
> Three miles further down the road a sign announces the way to Amberford and Oakfield. But what happened to Sticksbridge? (The map, securely tucked away in the glove compartment knows that Sticksbridge is six miles past Bigglesthwaite, which everyone around here knows is just down the road from Oakfield.) Next adventure: a fork in the road. Amberford is down the right fork. Oakfield is advertised for the left. But where's Sticksbridge? And then, surprise! Your perseverance, and your lucky guess at the fork pays dividends. A sign, hidden behind some leafy trees, informs you that Sticksbridge is indeed this way. (They could not have found a more awkward place to put this sign, even if they had tried.) Ten minutes later, you finally reach Sticksbridge, but not thanks to the signposting!

The less a service depends on human behaviour, the more important it is to define and quantify quality standards. Otis Elevator promises equipment repair within two hours, twenty four hours a day, seven days a week, and a phone call is all it takes to mobilize the engineers. The quality of service in the 'elevator' business is expressed in terms of speed, acceleration, deceleration, stopping, sound and light level.

American Express has defined two standards for its credit card: a 24-hour response to every credit card application and 'zero defect' on the card itself.

Club Med has defined precise quality service standards for the behaviour of its GOs, using words like courtesy, imagination, kindness, attention and generosity. These standards are used in recruiting as well as in training.

The National Westminster Bank has standards for answering requests for credit, which include not only the financial criteria, but also style and tone of the response.

A standard need not be absolute to be effective. It must simply express a commitment with regard to the promise made to the customer. For example, American Airlines defined a standard for baggage losses: fewer than 1200 per month. Sounds arbitrary or extremely liberal? Not at all. Its closest competitor loses nearly 1300.

## Service quality standards must be understood and applied throughout the organization

Service quality standards must be operational throughout an organization. Lufthansa, for example, makes this statement in its service promise: 'Businessmen want to get where they're going, not wait'. Converted into standards, the message to management becomes: 'The passenger must not wait more than thirty minutes at each step of his trip'. Management must therefore consider all of the elements which might effect the length of a stop-over: flight schedules, flight time, baggage check-in, baggage claim services, etc. Every employee in the baggage-handling department is guided by the same standard, whether he checks the suitcases, unloads them or drives the baggage tractor. (See Figure 6.1.)

The closer the standard gets to the person who actually serves the public, the more its components must be broken down into specific requirements. This practice will ensure the fullest customer satisfaction.

Every employee has to understand how his/her specific job contributes to creating a better service.

In a typical scenario there will be around 50 service quality standards for general management and about 1000 for the departments which contribute directly to service quality. These standards constitute the backbone of the company's service quality and are also a good indication of the company's service know-how.

The standards are further useful for training programmes. Too often the result expected by the customer is omitted from seminars which prefer to concentrate on operations (set a table, repair a machine, prepare a stage, etc.).

Comprehensive understanding of the standards can contribute to employee morale. The employee who understands the importance of his specific job will generally take pride in doing it better.

| General standard | Specific standards | |
|---|---|---|
| Company promise (service quality general standard) | Quality standards for luggage service | Quality standards for the luggage handler |

The passengers will have their luggage delivered to the pick-up point in less than fifteen minutes

| Tasks to be accomplished | How (method) | Result for the customer |
|---|---|---|
| Position the carts x minutes before the arrival<br>Unload the containers in order | Obtain flight information | Passengers are able to pick up their luggage in less than fifteen minutes |

| Tasks to be accomplished | How (method) | Result for the customer |
|---|---|---|
| Place the cart as close as possible to the conveyor belt | Approach from the front | Passengers can pick up their luggage in less than fifteen minutes |

*Figure 6.1 Service quality standards*

## Train personnel in quality standards

Standards must be communicated. They must be disseminated throughout the company. There are two ways of doing this: training and coaching.

British Airways organized a three-day course to disseminate the details of its new service quality standards. The programme reached each of the airlines' 30,000 employees. Club Med created number of six-day seminars to similarly inform its two thousand village managers, which amounted to an eight-months operation, as each seminar was limited to 50 people. Singapore Airlines insists on 12 weeks of training before a flight attendant meets her first customer.

Coaching has made many restaurant and hotel companies more successful. A department manager can, for instance, demonstrate a procedure. He will then monitor the employee while the latter performs the same procedure and correct his errors on the spot. The coach must obviously have excellent communication and demonstration skills and he must have time to devote to the trainee.

Investment in training will pay long-term dividends by ensuring compliance with quality standards.

Although classroom training is less risky than on-the-job training, the effective trainer never forgets the maxim:

**A person remembers:**

10% of what he reads,
20% of what he hears,
30% of what he sees,
50% of what he hears and sees,
70% of what he says and does,
90% of what is explained while it is being done.

While some people are born with a sense of service, others have to work to acquire one. The competitive CEO should ask himself how much the company is investing annually to train telephone operators, delivery drivers, reception hostesses, and counter clerks in comparison with the amount invested in training bookkeepers; how much time is devoted to making certain that the quality standards are clear and understandable.

## Delivering a customer-oriented service

Once the service quality standards are specified, the process of defining the relevant components begins. Four elements come into play:

- the people who provide the service,
- the equipment and machines which accompany the service,
- the procedures and methods to be followed to furnish the service, and
- the raw materials used in the service.

Suppose a department store decides to develop a competitive edge based on welcome, comfort and convenience, and freedom of choice. It will have to study flow patterns and interior decor (equipment), provide a large variety of brands (raw materials), design methods for welcoming/informing the customer and managing inventory (procedures and methods), and select and retrain sales staff, cashiers, reception and information personnel (the people).

A broad smile will not be enough to ensure a competitive advantage. Nor will pretty paintwork. The entire organization must be redesigned to address the service goal. The standard is only the starting point of an implementation policy which must affect each and every dimension of the firm. Quality does not tolerate approximation. Every detail must be considered. That is why it is so difficult to device a successful service quality policy. The receptionist's smile, broad though it may be, will never be able to compensate for an overloaded telephone system. Incidentally, implementation problems are *not* the customer's problem. He could not care less if delivery times are not respected because the widget factory is on strike.

Management can develop a set of procedures to deal with a late-widget problem. The first step should stress honesty. The customer should be told why his order is delayed and why the company is proposing an alternate supplier. Secondly, someone should be made responsible for managing the transaction. This person should personally take the unfilled order in hand and try to get it filled. If an alternate source of supply cannot be located, the customer should either be reimbursed for any prepaid charges, or offered an alternative solution. (The alternative solution should be considered even if it would involve a loss on the sale.) If all else fails, the complaint manager might want to consider parting with a part of his personal collection of widgets. The customer will be impressed with the extraordinary effort expended on his behalf, and will probably be a customer for a long time to come. If there is no alternative solution, any explanation may be insufficient. The customer may be dissatisfied, and a dissatisfied service customer may well be an ex- customer.

In order to monitor quality at the moment of service, it is necessary to list the various steps through which the customer passes to acquire the service. At each step, customer expectations must be defined and converted into quality standards. The error possibilities of each step must be identified and compared to the resources available to prevent repetition. (See Figure 6.2.)

| The steps through which the customer passes | ⇨ | ⇨ | ⇨ | ⇨ |
|---|---|---|---|---|
| What can go wrong?<br><br>Ways and means<br>• people<br>• methods<br>• equipment<br>• materials | ? | ? | ? | ? |

*Figure 6.2 The analysis of quality*

This method will probably surprise companies who prefer staring into space rather than concentrate on their customer. They will discover that service orientation consists of asking the customer:

- what his credit problem is *before* the name of his father and mother.
- what he wants to buy *before* his payment conditions.
- where he hurts *before* his insurance policy number.
- if he has an urgent job *before* his address and telephone.

The method is equally valid for organizing leisure activities as it is for delivering mail. DHL developed a letter delivery system which ensures its service quality. Each piece of mail passes through a number of stages on its way to final delivery. For each of these stages possible errors are anticipated and each handler is provided with the resources to correct them, on the spot.

American Hospital Supply designed a computer program to provide its customer with a user-friendly and efficient order system. (It typically costs a hospital about 50 pounds to place an order. These costs are mainly administrative and do not include the storage cost which are difficult to measure since many articles are immediately dispersed throughout the various departments.) Thanks to continuous computer-to-computer contact, hospitals can now place several orders per day, at minimal cost. Excessive paperwork and large inventories are no longer necessary.

Everything is recorded in the American Hospital Supply data base. The hospital administration accesses the AHS data base to find out how many operating room masks it has on hand. An innovative application of a commonplace technology has provided AHS with a competitive service edge. The shared screen technique monitors the customer's inventory and provides him an efficient, easy-to-use order system at the same time.

Today, computers can be used to record the volume of calls received/on hold and the average number of rings per call. With a bit of ingenuity, quality management is possible!

## Motivate personnel: a convinced employee is a convinced customer

Effective internal communications can also serve multiple purposes. They can be used to inform employees about quality standards and about the company's promise to the customer. The employee can gain a better understanding of how his contribution fits into the bigger picture.

Communication can also stimulate pride and mobilize enthusiasm. Many service oriented firms create advertising campaigns starring company personnel. A few years ago, to conclude a company quality improvement programme, British Airways introduced a new poster, picturing its stewards . . . as Supermen. Nevertheless, there are companies which refuse to spotlight their employees. They are wrong.

To sell the customer on its service quality, a company must first make sure its employees are sold on it. A sceptical employee will not convince a customer. The best companies launch full-fledged internal campaigns to sell their personnel on the desired level of excellence. These campaigns not only ensure an indispensable continuity in communication, but also have the effect of stimulating pride and morale.

A successful campaign must begin with a clear, 'catchy' slogan. This slogan must capture the essence of the campaign.

The company must organize a series of events which reinforce good service behaviour. Complementary letters from managers, articles in the company newsletter, regular quality meetings, awards which honour initiatives, contests for the best welcome of the month, the best repair job, election of a 'service champion' are just a few ideas. *Personnel must be made to understand the importance of quality.*

SAS, the Swedish airline, was losing seventy million dollars a year before Jan Carlson took over as CEO. Fifteen months later, it broke all profit records. Carlson does not attribute the recovery to his clairvoyance. He understood that the destiny of SAS was not in his hands, but in those of its twenty thousand employees. He met with them all to tell them: 'From now on, SAS is the businessman's European airline. Here are the general guidelines of this policy. Now it is up to you.'

In order to ease the pains associated with its recent merger with Piedmont Airlines, USAir instituted an employee information Hot Line. Employees can call it from anywhere in the world. A series of trunk dialings provide information on health benefits, new flight destinations, or the latest news about the company, its plans, and its accomplishments. This is an excellent way to reaffirm the company credo!

This chapter should leave the reader with one unimpeachable conclusion: a service orientation, adopted throughout a delivery system, can be a source of significant savings.

## THREE EXAMPLES OF QUALITY ANALYSIS

### Example 1 The sailboard at Club Méditerranée

**Service strategy:**

freedom of choice
quickly take advantage of the village

**Service quality standards:**

continuous 'self service' sports activities from 9 am to 5 pm with a course from 9 to 11 am and from 2 pm to 4 pm for those who wish it;
security assured;
be able to have a board within 15 minutes;
be able to use it for at least one hour.

**Service delivery system:**

a welcome;
the boards and accessories are available;
a lifeguard boat;
information about weather conditions and any dangers (rocks, currents, sea conditions).

**Quality analysis:**

*1 What are the steps a client goes through with their corresponding service standards?*

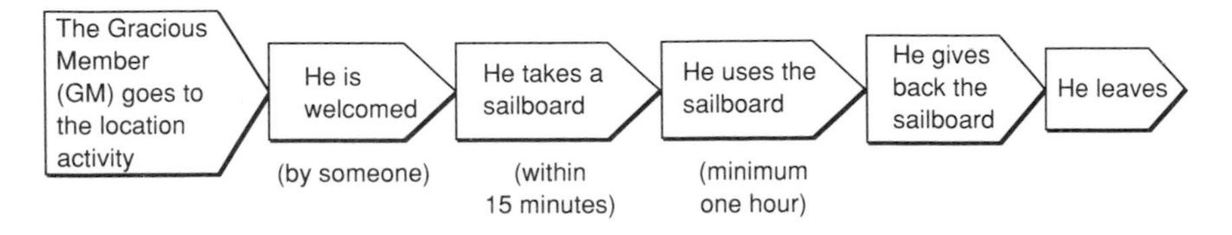

*2 What can make each step go wrong?*

| | | | | | |
|---|---|---|---|---|---|
| • Complicated schedules<br>• Location poorly indicated<br>• Location difficult to get to | • No welcome<br>• Cold and unpleasant welcome<br>• No information about the dangers<br>• No recommen-dations about the type of sailboard to use | • No board<br>• Board in poor condition<br>• It is decided that he cannot leave without a lesson<br>• The GM can not carry the board alone | • Equipment broken<br>• Board sinks<br>• The GM cannot come back alone<br>• The GM gets sunburnt | • The GM must return the board before the hour is over<br>• He cannot carry it by himself<br>• He must clean it<br>• He dismantles it and someone takes it<br>• He returns far from the starting point and must carry it | • Possession lost<br>• No goodbye |

*3 To ensure quality, what are the resources in methods, people, materials and equipment?*

| | | | | | |
|---|---|---|---|---|---|
| **People** | • Number of GOs<br>• Training of GOs | • Assistance | • Safety | • Assistance | • Courtesy<br>• Safety |
| **Material**<br>• Posting of panels<br>• Direction panels<br>• Orientation panels | | | • Life guard boat<br>• Sun screen cream | | |
| **Equipment**<br>• Pathways cleared | | • No extra equipment | | • Better boards<br>• More boards | • Safety |
| **Methods**<br>• Schedule planning | • Finding information and communica-tion of information | • Interview<br>• Choice of material | • Choice of material | • Sailboard maintenance<br>• Test/evalua-tion of experience | |

**Example 2 The DHL service**

**Service strategy:** deliver company mail within 24 hours or 48 hours to any place on the world.

**Service quality standards:** delivery within 24 hours;
without errors;
without damage (safety);
accessible during office hours.

**Service delivery system:** collection points easily accessible to the customer;
dispatching (sorting, sending);
an arrival collection point.

**Quality analysis:**

*1 The steps*

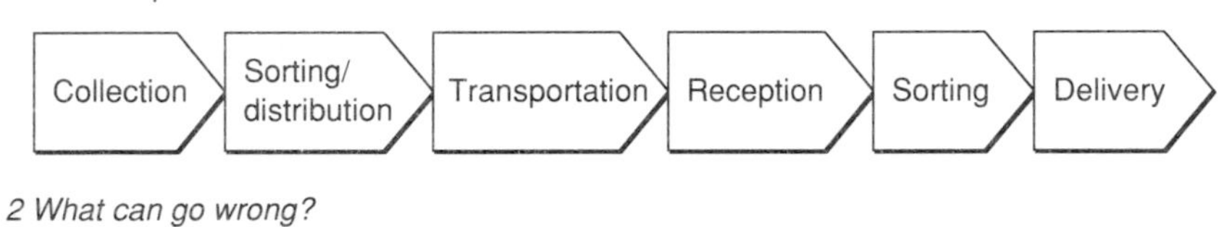


*2 What can go wrong?*

| Collection | Sorting/distribution | Transportation | Reception | Sorting | Delivery |
|---|---|---|---|---|---|
| • Address unknown<br>• Too many people<br>• Bad welcome<br>• Poor knowledge of rates<br>• Loss of mail | • Losses<br>• Thefts<br>• Bad orientation<br>• Illegible address<br>• Damage<br>• Slowness | • Late timing<br>• Losses<br>• Thefts<br>• Damage | • Delay in customs<br>• Losses<br>• Thefts<br>• Damage | • Errors<br>• Delays<br>• Damage<br>• Losses | • Errors<br>• Delays<br>• Damage<br>• Losses |

*3 The resources*

| | Collection | Sorting/distribution | Transportation | Reception | Sorting | Delivery |
|---|---|---|---|---|---|---|
| **People** | • More personnel trained for receiving customers | • Training for sorting | | • Negotiation with customs | | |
| **Equipment** | • Location of shops | • Automation of sorting/ distribution | • Choice of transportation companies | | | |
| **Material** | | | • Containers | | | |
| **Methods/ procedures** | • Procedure followed<br>• Scheduling based upon activity | • Sorting method<br>• Protection<br>• Identification of letters | • Negotiations with airlines<br>• Insurance | | | |

### Example 3 Microcomputer sales

**Service strategy:** give the customers the best availability in the whole industry

**Quality standards:** repair service 5 days out of 7, 10 hours per day, on the dealer's premises;
if the breakdown is not found after one hour, moving up to headquarters;
if, at the end of six hours, the computer is not repaired, the ongoing work is taken over on another computer, or another computer is lent.

**Quality analysis:**

*1 The steps*

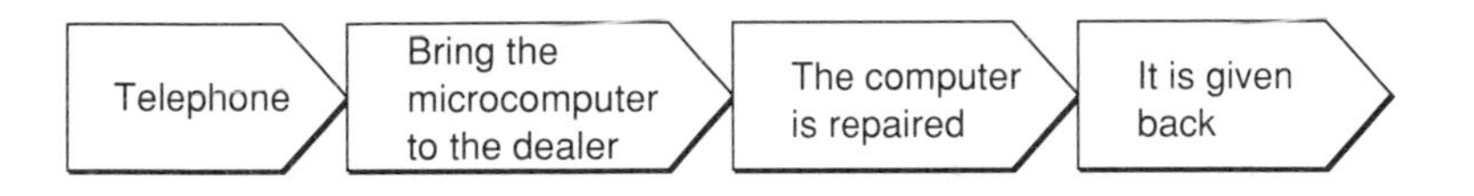


*2 What can go wrong?*

| | | | |
|---|---|---|---|
| • No answer<br>• Not friendly, not personalized<br>• Not routed to the right person<br>• Telephone busy<br>• Poor knowledge of the particular model | • Does not know the details of the repair<br>• Cannot give an idea of price<br>• Does not ask the right questions to find the cause<br>• Bad welcome | • No parts available<br>• Does not succeed in identifying the cause<br>• Not enough people for the repair | • It doesn't work<br>• No explanation why repair is impossible<br>• Exorbitant invoice<br>• Erroneous invoice<br>• Doesn't notify customer when the computer is repaired |

*3 The ways and means*

| | | | | |
|---|---|---|---|---|
| **People** | | | | |
| | • Training repairman for receiving customers | • Training in diagnosis, welcome preparing invoice | • Training | |
| **Equipment** | | | | |
| | • Telephone switchboard | | • Machines available<br>• Spare parts | • Loan of machines |
| **Materials** | | | | |
| | • Documentation to be clarified | | | |
| **Methods** | | | | |
| | • Methods for routing the customer | • Information about time necessary to repair<br>• Know-how about invoices | • Methods for diagnosis, monitoring and scheduling the repair | • Invoicing<br>• Inspection and testing<br>• Notifying customer |

## Self-diagnosis

- Do you have service quality standards?
- How many?
- Are they expressed in terms of results for the customer?
- Do they include tasks and the method for getting these results?
- Are they suitable in their formulation and their scope for each level of personnel?
- Does everybody know them?
- Are they measurable?
- Do they correspond to your promise, to your service strategy?
- In your training programmes, before teaching the tasks to be performed and the methods, is everyone reminded how this serves the customer?
- Is your service delivery system customer oriented? Or is it more oriented to the inside of the company?
- Are your employees convinced of the service quality of your company? Have you tried to convince them? With the same care and effort that you give to your external communications?

# 7

# The Error Hunt: a Quest for Zero Defect

Quality defects never escape customer scrutiny. In a service industry, zero defect is not a luxury. It is a necessity. The idea of 'zero defect' must be studied in relation to the level of service and the quality standards identified by the company. Zero defect is a relative concept.

When American Airlines loses fewer than 1200 pieces of luggage items per month, the quality standard which it has set for itself, it reaches 'zero defect'. Its closest competitor loses nearly 1300 pieces. Hence there is no need to try and obtain a zero-loss rate. The cost would be prohibitive. A standard with a zero luggage-loss rate would only become necessary if, due to word of mouth, the cost of passenger desertion became greater than the cost of indemnification.

'Do it right first time'. This is the surest way to reach zero defect in service quality. It is impossible to erase an error once the service has been rendered.

## Do it right first time

'Doing it right first time' is a matter of attitude. The employee who will most readily buy into the idea is one who:

- likes what he's doing; (It is very difficult, if not impossible, to expect someone to do something right first time if he does not feel comfortable with his job. The nature of the work is also important. It helps if complexity and gratification factors of the job correspond to worker expectations.)
- has pride in his work. (Pride is a major consideration for every person in direct contact with the customer.)

Granada Motorways Services increased its sales by 25 per cent by practicing the 'do it right first time' in their toilet areas. Each attendant was issued an attractive, new uniform, a chair and a table. Each was trained to warmly welcome customers with a personalized touch. The toilet areas were rearranged to include a spacious coatroom and clean premises. Results? Customers spend more time (and money) in the station. At the Bermuda Onion, a fashionable Paris restaurant, the waitresses' changing rooms are designed like film-star dressing rooms, complete with costume wardrobes, individual make-up tables, mirrors, neon lighting and stage settings. The Bermuda Onion waitresses feel like film stars. They welcome like stars and they serve like stars.

Pride is not only a question of ethics. It also results from how a person thinks he is perceived by his peers. Many factors can increase staff pride and therefore its willingness to 'do it right first time', i.e., uniforms, badges, internal communications, a review process, the stature given to relationships with customers, the manner in which the staff is addressed.

## A total commitment to one's work

Zero defect requires discipline and a total commitment in one's work. The rate of absenteeism in Japan is 3 per cent. In Great Britain it is 15 per cent.

Singapore Airlines recruits three hundred flight attendants every year. Its training programme is twelve weeks long. Tardy arrival at three training sessions disqualifies a candidate. Message sent, message received!

## Enthusiasm

Finally, zero defect is a question of enthusiasm. A recent study showed that enthusiastic people have the following characteristics:

- they are sensitive to compliments from the customer and motivated by such compliments;
- they feel that their company is providing support and allowing freedom to take initiatives in the field.

A company can have a great influence on these two attributes. The individual's sensitivity to compliment can be identified at the time of recruitment and nourished by the company. Management has only to facilitate letters of congratulations from customers and pass them on to the responsible party. It might be possible to extend the interaction time between the contact personnel and customers, giving the customer time to express satisfaction. For example, on short flights, an airline might limit its services in order to give the crew time to chat with the passengers and for the passengers to compliment them.

To select enthusiastic contact personnel, many companies have developed tests subjecting the candidates to real working situations. A video shows a customer in a hurry. He wants to be served before the others. Candidates' responses are observed. Test situations should be those similar to those occurring frequently on-the-line and designed to identify enthusiastic behaviour. It is equally important for management to make certain that employees who have already proven themselves are not slighted in the process. USAir issues future flight attendants with a series of manuals which specify the nature of the work, the quality levels demanded and all service procedures, and asks them to read the contents carefully. Some candidates are intimidated by the thickness of the manuals and resign from the programme. Those losses are easily offset by the guarantee of quality delivered by those who overcome this initial stumbling block.

Contact personnel also need to feel that their decisions will be supported by management. When they feel secure, the results can be astonishing.

> A village manager at Club Med had prepared, according to custom, a Christmas Eve celebration. Also according to custom, he invited some local dignitaries. The locals arrived in greater numbers than expected and it was soon apparent that there was not going to be enough food. The village manager asked the Gracious Members to join him in welcoming the guests. For their trouble and for the unexpected problems, a second Christmas dinner would be served to them the following day. Favourably impressed, many Gracious Members returned to the village for repeat visits, which meant more business.

The village manager's initiative would not have been possible if he thought it would be censured.

In a recent British Airways survey, passengers identified the two service criteria which they considered most important when travelling abroad. The first one was flexibility. Passengers wanted to know that the airline would help them organize alternative travel solutions in case of problems. Next, passengers were concerned about compensation, i.e., the manner in which they would be indemnified for inconvenience due to company error.

It is therefore essential that a company delegates certain prerogatives to the contact personnel in order to enable them to take initiatives and to rectify any situation which deviates from service quality standards. Agents, reception personnel, deliverymen, technicians, hotel managers, and customer representatives serve in the front lines. They must know what initiatives they can take on their own. Having front-line personnel list the initiative they can take 'without' and 'only-with' prior authorization may be revealing. If they have to seek approval too often they may not have the tools to properly serve their customers. Without flexibility, contact staff can only respond with evasive answers. Evasive answers mean frustrated customers.

'Doing it right first time' may require a major investment in recruitment, selection, training and stimulation of personnel. The cost should nevertheless not be a prohibiting factor. Non-quality is more expensive, as the following example shows:

> A firm needed reception personnel to work at various European sites. The task involved several steps: recruitment of candidates, analysis of dossiers, pre-selection, interviews, final selection, assignment of the candidate and acceptance by the person responsible at the site.
>
> As standard practice, the firm studied application letters, with or without curriculum vitae, submitted in response to a newspaper advertisement. They selected a number of candidates for interviews. Immediately after the interviews, the best applicants were sent directly to the job site. Result? Twenty per cent resigned before the end of the first month. Amount wasted: £400,000.

The responsibility for this loss was shared by three departments: Recruitment, Personnel and Site Management.

Yet the £400,000 were not the only loss. Most of the 20 per cent who resigned performed poorly while on the job. The newcomers were not prepared for their duties. They grew angry with the firm and, as often happens, passed their anger on to the customers.

This attrition could have been avoided. The firm should first of all have defined the recruitment criteria. The initial screening should have been standardized. A basic, service-oriented test should have enabled more rigorous pre-selection. Interviewers should have known more about the nature of the work and the skills required. Site managers should have been made part of the final selection process. A welcome booklet should have informed the newcomers about job requirements and behaviour standards. The new employees should have been assigned to a training programme.

Had all of these alternatives been instituted, the cost would have been far less than £400,000. 'Doing it right first time' may not be cost-free, but it is always cheaper than sub-par work.

## Zero defect entails an uncompromising error chase

### Track down and chase errors

The error chase consists of tracking down, classifying, analysing and correcting all the deviations from quality standards. Before the chase begins, two points demand attention.

Firstly, the error chase should not become a witch hunt. The discovery of a conformity deviation should end in corrective action, not in blame. Employees will not participate in an error chase if they think they will be punished for the anomalies. Next, the error chase must include everyone who has contact with the customer. Do not call in the KGB. The error chase must be perceived as a constructive management approach.

An error chase should also include all the service elements, methods, procedures, equipment, and tasks which do not deliver their part of the quality promise. The chase should be spontaneous and informal. There should be no need to establish a quality circle to pick up a scrap of paper on a hotel lobby floor. That's everybody's job. Picking up papers is not the exclusive domain of the cleaning personnel. When the telephone rings, everyone should feel concerned. The person nearest the phone should answer. No need to wait for the receptionist to come back from lunch.

In some cases, the error chase involves major, more complex problems requiring substantial modifications to company procedures. An investment may be involved. Several company departments may be affected by the change. In such cases, a formal error chasing procedure must be established.

### Organizing the error chase

Most error chases are initiated by a working group whose first assignment is to identify, list and classify errors. The next step involves a search for solutions based on available resources. Pivoting on this group, information traffic is organized vertically from bottom to top, to propose solutions and, from top to bottom, to approve suggested improvements.

The working groups may take three different forms: quality project teams, quality action squads or quality circles. Each group will have different types of assignments. The closer a service error is located in a detail of furnishing the service, the more urgent immediate and simple solutions are, and the more contact personnel needs to be included.

The quality circle will only be effective if management offers highly visible support. It is helpful if the idea of participation already exists in the firm's management structure. The circle concept will not work effectively if the company maintains an authoritarian posture in some matters and encourages participation in others.

It is also important that the circle leader be comfortable with his function, both in relation to management and to the group members. This person will benefit from training in active listening and group dynamics.Timely reward and recognition for tangible results will always improve the success of a quality circle. The circle leader should start the group with problems which are relatively simple to solve. The results can subsequently be published in the house journal. It goes without saying that the group must receive the backing and support of management. (The more the problems to be addressed effect the bottom line, the more management will want to be involved.) Management also has the responsibility of defining the quality standards which the circle will address, as well as the scope of the error chase.

At Club Med, the error chase programme began only after management approved the quality standards and set them down in a 1200 page book.

## Error chase: everyone's obsession, every instant

In an interview with *International Management Magazine*, the CEO of the Mövenpick hotel chain pointed out that it is a mistake to think that service quality and customer satisfaction are ever definitively acquired. The process is an on-going one. In the frequent two-day meetings which he organizes with his staff, such detailed matters as the clarity of the instructions to be followed in case of theft or fire, new coat hangers, and guests' jogging cards are often discussed. He sends fictitious application letters to the personnel department to study the speed and quality of the responses. Several times a year, he checks with guests to test the quality of the hotel service.

## Suggestions moving up and responses moving down: the role of the Quality Manager

The working group needs a system to facilitate the communication of employee suggestions and the decisions taken by management. Many companies appoint a Quality Manager to manage this traffic. Others have formed Quality Committees. The advantage of the latter is that management can participate in the process from the beginning. The Committee examines proposals and passes them on to the Quality Director for follow-up.

The Quality Manager is a facilitator. He reports to management and manages correspondents in the various units, divisions, departments or sections of the organization. His responsibilities are many.

*He must facilitate the quality improvement process.* He will assist operational people in the formulation of quality standards and attempt to procure the concurrence of general management. He will facilitate the distribution of the standards throughout the organization. *He may be called upon to design a format* in which the standards can be written, edit them and create dissemination methods. At the request of general management, he may help the working groups with planning. Finally, he will participate in cost assessment and help identify the benefits of the solutions.

*He must represent and defend his customer's point of view.* He designs and conducts the customer satisfaction survey, and he makes sure that its results are distributed within the company. By emphasizing the results of the survey, he helps the departments define service delivery standards. He represents the customer's point of view in all management meetings. He manages inquiries into specific points of service.

*He performs quality audits.* In his audit function, the Quality Director acts neither as an inspector nor as a policeman. He runs the audits in close coordination with department managers. With them, he summarizes the results which he then communicates to general management.

*He prepares the service quality training tools and manages training programmes.* He is the quality advocate. He stimulates the spirit of quality, everyday and everywhere. He encourages innovation. He circulates articles, personal reports and results within the company. He tests competitive services and communicates the results. He records internal innovations, creates contests and chooses quality winners. He guides innovative projects during their preliminary phases. He proposes progress producing projects to management.

*He is the company's quality spokesman to the outside world.* He joins trade associations, participates in conferences, gives speeches and grants interviews concerning the company's experience in the service quality field.

The Quality Manager has no formal authority. He must rely on influence and persuasion. In order to be credible, he must prove that he deserves to be considered a 'mentor', respected for his contributions, and he must act with the unconditional support of management.

The Quality Manager must create a network of correspondents within the company, in order to collect relevant data. His correspondents may help him prepare the error chase training tools.

No need to set up a quality management bureaucracy. One full-time person can do the job. He can establish an informal network of contacts and correspondents to assure in-put from all relevant departments. That's all. At IBM-France, for example, the team responsible for quality management consists of a manager and three assistants.

## The error chase and time

To sustain motivation and enthusiasm in the error chase, it is imperative that the ideas which are submitted to management receive immediate attention and quick response. Receipt of each idea should be acknowledged within 48 hours and a response should be returned within 30 days. Some companies handle 300 to 1000 recommendations each year.

One way of ensuring speedy action is to allocate operational management a small budget which they can use to finance quality projects. Formal steps and procedures can be by-passed. The truly innovative idea may not wait until next year!

An error chase will include:

- the error targeted,
- an analysis of the causes, a list of possible solutions,
- a detailed explanation of the recommended solution,
- results of experimentation (if the solution needs to be tested),

- the present total cost of the non-quality,
- the total cost at 'zero defect',
- the expected investment,
- the consequences for other parts of the company,
- the projected time for the project to become profitable.

## The error chase begins with customer service

To achieve consistent quality, it is obviously important to examine the company's internal services, as well as the services provided to the customer. Many companies linger over the former to the detriment of the latter.

Internal services must be evaluated in light of their contributions to outside services. They cannot be ends in themselves. Any error chase begins with the customer. Customer expectations should define the demands which departments make on each other.

In the 1970s, many companies suffered from a 'dialogue of the deaf' with centralized computer departments whose functions related more to bookkeeping than to management. It often demanded a great deal of shouting, with proof in hand that customer-based demands were not being met before data processing supervisors would choose to be responsive. Customer expectations will produce agreement between sales and production managements, between research scientists and treasurers, between financial controllers and division managers.

Front-line employees receive a genuine stimulus when the process begins by studying customer satisfaction. They will be better motivated if their efforts result in increased sales than if they are merely thanked for being nice to the other departments.

Managers should reread procedure manuals and inter-departmental documents to make certain that they all address the needs of the customers. Many will be surprised at the number of procedures, documents and rules which never mention *them.*

## The tools for the error chase

Industry has already designed tools to improve product quality. With minor adaptations, many of these tools can be used in the search for service quality.

An error chase has two phases: identifying errors and seeking causes. Some industry tools can be applied at each phase.

### *Identifying errors*

Some industry tools can be used to detect and classify errors. Brainstorming sessions, suggestion boxes, complaint letter analysis, classifying reimbursements by cause, and user surveys are a few examples. All these will provide you with a list of errors which must then be classified and prioritized.

The best known method for establishing a hierarchy of errors is the Pareto analysis. Each error is assigned a coefficient indicating its magnitude. The Quality Group must then tackle the errors in order of importance.

The relative weight of errors is defined using criteria similar to those employed in manufacturing. Instead of calculating the frequency of rejects during production or counting the number of pieces which do not pass inspection, for example, a service programme will calculate the frequency of late deliveries, the frequency of repairs, reimbursements, the number of telephone rings per call and/or the number of files mislaid.

Unfortunately, not all services lend themselves to measurement. One cannot measure the 'frequency' of a smile, for example. Some managers therefore prefer to use a point system. Starting with a predetermined number of points, say 100, group members are asked to list errors and assign point values. The total of the values cannot exceed 100.

It is necessary, though, that group members agree on the criteria by which errors are classified. Frequency is not always a valid indicator. It is equally important to avoid reasoning by averages. Market sectors must be clearly identified since different sectors may have different expectations. The advertiser who devotes one million pounds to his advertising campaign does not have the same expectations as the one who spends 100 thousand pounds. The customer who buys thirty computers does not have the same requirements as the customer who buys three. When listing errors, weight must be modified accordingly.

### *Seeking causes*

Causes must be identified before solutions can be defined. They can be tracked down by utilizing the Ishikawa diagram, the 'fishbone' analysis. Causes are identified by sampling the service. This is a particularly effective approach when the service is rendered at several locations. The solution process begins by systematically modifying one variable at a time. Such a trial makes it possible to test the situation before adopting a definitive solution.

Looking at the bibliography, the reader will notice that a whole range of tools exists. Each has built-in advantages and disadvantages, but each tool has to be used systematically. Being systematic avoids discussions in a vacuum, unfounded disagreements and lost time. Participants must understand the importance of the process and not see it as a theoretical exercise. The goal is to provide more and better satisfaction to customers!

## Self-diagnosis

- Do your service people like what they are doing? Are they proud? Are they enthusiastic?
- What have you done in terms of selection, training, motivation to make them proud of their work?
- How much independent authority is granted to employees in contact with the customer? What is it that they cannot do?
- Do you have tests for selecting those enthusiastic about providing service?
- Do your employees ever receive letters of praise?
- Do you have an organized error-chase procedure?
- If it has already started, is your quality programme more oriented toward external or internal quality?

# 8

# Measuring Customer Satisfaction

The customer's perception of a service quality is often different from the perception of the provider. This difference in perception is caused by a number of factors.

Firstly there may be a misunderstanding about the criterion applied. A consulting firm recently organized a seminar in one of those *chateaux* modified for this purpose. The organizer had been assured that the participants would enjoy the best of service during the coffee break, i.e., porcelain dishes and real silverware, tablecloths, an assortment of biscuits, coffee and tea, costumed waiters with many platters and many smiles. Quite sure of himself, the organizer later asked the participants to judge the service quality of the coffee break. He was stupefied to learn that 80 per cent of the participants were dissatisfied. He had not realized that the executives wanted telephones and toilets during break time.

A company can also become the prisoner of its own language. House jargon is often used to measure the quality of the service offered, but it may be unsuitable to measure the quality of service purchased. For example:

| the firm conceives and measures: | the customer perceives and measures: |
|---|---|
| the range of the product line | the extent of the choice and the counsel |
| the lay-out of the display cases and the number of running meters of display | the presence of merchandise |
| a credit card accepted by the merchants | spontaneous gifts |
| architectural and design specifications | comfort and convenience |
| the premium conditions and payment schedules | the advantages of the insurance contract |

A company's obsession with internal organization can constitute another substantial distortion. It is a rare company that places itself in the customer's position when measuring satisfaction. Some companies even consider the customer a nuisance. What savings could be made if *he* was not there! Unfortunately, without *him,* there would be no company.

Finally, a company may believe that its service is so unique that there is no basis for comparison. This company *assumes* that the customer will be satisfied. After all, if the company is the world's only producer of left-handed widgets, why should it worry about customer satisfaction? The fallacy: customers may find ways to adapt right handed widgets or build their products without using any widgets at all.

Consumer surveys are very revealing in this respect. In one such survey, published in 1986 in '50 *Millions de Consommateurs*' (the French consumer report), consumers were asked to rate the services of national utilities against private sector firms. The National Electricity Company received an 82 per cent satisfaction rating, followed by the National Telephone Company with 80 per cent, the National Railroad and the National Post Office, each with 75 per cent. Similar levels of satisfaction with such public services are reported in the UK and other European countries. Hospitals, whose services require considerably more interaction for longer periods, received a rating of 53 per cent. McDonald's scored a flashy 95 per cent.

Although we suggested earlier that an alarm should go off when satisfaction rates fall below 80 per cent; a durable competitive advantage requires an average of at least 94 per cent.

## Satisfaction surveys

There is a simple way to learn about customer satisfaction. Ask the customer about his feelings, ask him regularly, track the changes and measure the progress.

A successful survey begins with a good questionnaire, and a good questionnaire is always built from the customer's point of view. The objective of such a questionnaire is to optimally gauge the customer's feelings, and not to bombard him with questions about matters which do not concern him or about which he has never reflected.

Hence, to build an effective questionnaire, it is indispensable to begin with a qualitative phase.

Individual or group interviews will give an indication of the customer's concerns, expectations and language. A strong data base will include information gathered from former, current, and potential customers. The questions, which are based on interviews, will then focus on the various aspects of quality which are important to the buyer. Survey results on their own are not very illuminating. Once results are collected, they must be compared with the results of the competition or, if that is not possible, with the quality perceived for an analogous service. An 80 per cent satisfaction rate is less acceptable when management learns that the competition rates 90 per cent. It goes without saying that a difference favouring the competitor demands a more energetic response than would a slight drop in satisfaction.

Satisfaction measurements may be taken daily, weekly, monthly or annually. Everything depends upon purchase frequency and the speed with which the company can modify its quality programme

Club Med checks the satisfaction of its Gracious Members every week. It is able to rectify oversights immediately. Swissair performs monthly samplings. The results of the survey are submitted to the Chairman of the Board. The survey typically consists of questions such as: 'Did you have to wait more than or less than three minutes at check-in?' The questionnaire is given to randomly selected passengers, in an envelope upon which is written: 'The better we know your opinion, the better we can serve you'. This questionnaire, filled in with some 5,000 quality comments, is analysed every three months, and the results are compared to the quality measured in the field by the supervisor at each airport.

Xerox conducts annual surveys which monitors, among other items, after-sale service. The data are compared to the results of surveys the company automatically performs three months after an installation.

The renewal of a maintenance or insurance contract, the periodic statement from a building manager, bank or credit card company, a follow-up letter, all present opportunities to include a customer satisfaction survey. Cost need not be a prohibiting factor.

The sceptic may observe: 'Only unhappy customers answer' or 'We will just bother the customer' or 'The questionnaire will give the customer the wrong ideas'. It has never been demonstrated that a questionnaire unfavourably influenced a customer. It is more probable that some degree of dissatisfaction pre-dated the questionnaire. People seldom feel harassed when they feel they're contributing to research that will directly benefit them.

The survey must result in tangible action. A stack of questionnaires is only a pile of paper. Merely counting them is not enough. They must be studied in detail before they can return on investment.

Once the survey results are collated, they must be analysed. How does management know whether 20 per cent of dissatisfied customers means 20 per cent of customers lost or whether only a proportion of them have deserted the firm? How many of the 20 per cent dissatisfied customers will also bad-mouth the company.

To answer this type of question, 'buying behaviour' must be examined and the effect of word of mouth' measured. Only then can management begin to draw informed conclusions.

Research has shown that around 15 per cent of the dissatisfied customers were customers not targetted by this service and therefore impossible to satisfy at any rate. If the total dissatisfaction rate is 20 per cent, this means that only three per cent (15% of 20% = 3%) of the client base is irretrievably lost.

Finally, management may choose to identify a number of faithful customers. Interviews with faithful customers will provide data vital to analysing the attitude of the 'dissatisfieds'.

## Complaint letters: a source of profit

Surveys are not the only means by which to measure customer satisfaction. Complaint or compliment letters can also become quality management tools. Although these letters add a touch of detail which no survey can cover, they do not provide a basis for sound statistical analysis.

Few people take the effort to write and, understandably, unhappy customers comprise the larger percentage of the letter writers. Dissatisfied people tend to write more often than satisfied people. A company can expect to receive ten complaint letters for each compliment letter.

Carefully managed, the complaint letter can be a powerful tool. Between 55 per cent and 70 per cent of complaining customers will use a service again if they are answered quickly. The rate climbs to 95 per cent, if they are answered quickly and well. A quick response must be made in less than two weeks, preceded by an acknowledgement within 48 hours. A quick calculation shows that if a company receives one thousand letters per year and if they're answered *quickly* and *well*, 950 customers can be recovered. If each spends £500 a year, sales will increase by £50,000.

It should take no more than one-fourth of a person-year to answer the 1000 letters. The correspondent could easily become the most productive person in the company.

To recover 95 per cent of the unsatisfied customers, it is important, first of all, that the letters be properly processed. A 'lost' letter is definitely worse than no-letter-at-all. A very simple way to make certain that complaint letters receive proper attention is to tell customers *where* and *whom* to write. Include the information on all of the documents which leave the company, including invoices, monthly statements, packaging, advertising circulars, etc.. The best way to increase the number of letters is to have them sent to the manager. It is also an excellent way for the manager to remain in contact with the customers.

Imagine the following message at the bottom of a credit card statement:

'IF YOU ARE NOT SATISFIED, WRITE TO ME. I WILL ANSWER YOU.
Signed, The manager.'

A bad answer to a 'Letter of complaint' will include the following mistakes:

date: (very long after receipt of the complaint ---15 days to 3 months)

Dear Sir: (you have to keep your distance with a nuisances . . .)

1st paragraph: You may be right but I am still surprised because . . (You're too demanding, this does not usually happen and I do not really believe it happened to you)

2nd paragraph: Be assured that the responsible personnel will be punished . . . (Hopefully you'll feel guilty and end this correspondence in its tracks. You do not really like for people to be punished, do you?)

3rd paragraph: Anyway, I trust this will not effect our relationship (We're not really so bad, after all)

4th paragraph: I think I answered all your questions and I thank you for bringing the problem to my attention . . . (Do not bother me any more with this trivia. Do you think I do not know how to run this business?)

Signature

(A secretary signing for Mr X)

(The answer is from Mr X. The complaint was not even addressed to him. That really makes you feel important.)

A good answer will include the following elements:

> Date: (under 48 hours)
>
> Dear Client: (YOU're very important to us!)
>
> 1st paragraph: Thanks for taking the time to write . . . (After all, you did not have to. You could have switched to the competition and never bothered to tell me.)
>
> 2nd paragraph: You're right! We do not have any excuse and I take full responsibility . . . (The buck stops here! I'm the manager. I take the blame.)
>
> 3rd paragraph: This is what we're going to do to prevent the problem from happening again . . . ( I'll show you that your letter will get action.)
>
> 4th paragraph: Meanwhile I'd like to propose . . . (reimbursement, invitation for a free visit, more excuses . . . . )
>
> 5th paragraph: Do not hesitate to let me know the next time there's something wrong! By giving us your input you help us serve you better. (We want to hear from you.)
>
> Signature
> (The CEO in person)

Delta Airlines recently ran a black and white advertisement in the *New York Times*, displaying thirty photos of CEOs. Each was reading a letter. Twenty-nine were smiling. The thirtieth looked stern. The text under the stern-faced photo read: 'I read them all and I answer them all'.

Not many companies systematically encourage their customers to write to them. Fewer still supply an address. Yet the customer service department should easily be able to deal with these letters and reply, store them in memory, follow them up and analyse the results, with the help of word-processing equipment. When handling complaints, it is a good policy to exceed the customer's demand. Better to reimburse twenty five pounds for a twenty-pound demand than to lose 95 per cent of the unhappy customers. Forcing the customer to enter a verbal tug-of-war can be a risky business. One runs the risk of compromising other components of the company communications programme. The effect of an attractive advertising campaign will be negated if a customer cannot get a straight answer to his questions. Give the customer a contact point! Ikea, the furniture retailer, understands this. Next to each set of furniture on display, they install two small boxes and a pencil. In one, the buyer finds the order form; in the other, he finds an evaluation form. The customer has the feeling that somebody wants his opinion and that it will be taken seriously.

The more difficult it is for the customer to complain, the quieter dissatisfied customers will be. But, consider the four per cent answer rate. Multiply the number of complaint letters by one hundred and divide by four. The result is a good indication of the number of customers who can be categorized: 'exasperated'.

## The opinion of others

A company can track the rate at which a product is returned and measure the rate of repeat business. The opinions of personnel in direct contact with the customer are a precious source of information. These people often also hold the key to service solutions. Delivery staff, salespeople, repair staff, tellers and chambermaids, all encounter happy customers and unhappy customers. They are the only ones who know why the customers feel the way they do.

Although an 'image study' is generally used to assess the reputation of a firm or to measure the effectiveness of an advertising campaign, it can also cover customer satisfaction or, at least measure the way in which the existing and potential customers perceive the company's promise. However, an 'image study' tends to reveal the expectations of the market rather than the degree of satisfaction.

Finally, the number of dissatisfied customers can be assessed by counting the number of customers who have been reimbursed each year. Yet a reimbursed customer should not be confused with a dissatisfied customer. If the company has a very restrictive reimbursement policy, there may be more dissatisfied customers than reimbursed customers.

Putting oneself in the customer's position remains the most effective way to learn about the quality of a service. The executive might occasionally phone his own company. He can pose as a customer and ask for information. This is the fastest way to learn about service! If he wants to know if his delivery system is satisfactory, he can have something delivered to his neighbour or his in-laws. The results will have no statistical value, but they can give a good idea of what the customers are receiving.

Too many CEOs are content with the service supplied by their companies because they do not have to wait in line when they arrive at one of their hotels. They get immediate repair when they drive into one of the garages in their chain. They get a big smile when they walk into one of their department stores.

It is easy for facts to get obscured. In certain insurance policies, for example, the fine print mandates that to cancel the policy, a registered letter must be sent thirty days before the expiry date. If the notification is not received, the policy is automatically renewed. Although there are many people who are insured 'in spite of themselves', contract renewals often provide the basis by which some firms calculate satisfaction. In the same way, if only ten per cent of complaints are recognized, and if only ten per cent of the complaints are indemnified, the balance sheet will show a minimum number of refunds. If the refund rate is the standard by which the firm measures satisfaction, the company will – wrongfully – be very satisfied with itself.

To summarize, the level of excellence delivered does not necessarily correspond to customer perception. To know how the customer really feels, it is necessary to ask his opinion and to pose the question in a way that makes sense to him. It is also necessary to conduct surveys which are designed to minimize contamination. The results of surveys should be compared with the competition's results when possible. Satisfaction rates must be compared with 'repeat business' statistics. Even when a problem seems to be an exceptionally rare one, it must be taken seriously and fully investigated. Be assured: it is possible to know what the customer thinks, but sometimes it may take a bit of courage.

## Self-diagnosis

- Do you perform regular surveys to measure the satisfaction of your customers?
- What is the satisfaction rate of your customers?
- What was it last year? Two years ago?
- How do your results compare with those of the competition?
- What is the rate of repeat business for your service? For satisfied customers? For dissatisfied customers?
- How many customers do you lose each year?
- How many complaint letters do you receive each year? What is the ratio between the number of complaint letters and the number of dissatisfied customers?
- How many compliment letters do you receive each year?
- How much time do you take to answer complaints?
- Do you display compliment letters?
- Do you have a clear procedure, appropriately communicated, for the customer to express himself?

# 9

# Are you being Served?

While writing this book I decided to keep a record of my service quality experiences. I was convinced that I would meet situations of flawless and botched service in practically equal numbers.

As I reread the notebook in which I conscientiously set down my adventures, I discovered, to my stupefaction, that it contained mostly horror stories. Was fortune frowning on me? Was my eye particularly critical? One thing is sure; it is considerably easier to lose a customer than to win one.

It was very difficult to choose among the hundreds of stories shared by friends. I selected the ones that seemed the most instructive.

JH

**A major American airline**

One of the major American airlines is remodelling its departure desks. Half of them are closed and staffing has been reduced accordingly. To make things just perfect, three flights for New York are taking off at the same time. No need to draw pictures. Long lines form at the few open desks and my flight finally departs, forty-five minutes late.

**Moral:** The customer must pay twice for the overhaul of the desks, once by buying his ticket and a second time by missing his business appointment.

**The family restaurant**

An American restaurant chain has positioned itself as a 'family restaurant'. It offers a menu of old-style favourites (peanut butter, jelly and banana sandwiches, for example). The restaurant is famous for its white, paper, table covers. Each table is topped-off with a wine glass full of crayons. Customers, young and old alike, are invited to create masterpieces while waiting or between courses. Before any table cover is discarded, waiters are instructed to look for outstanding pieces of 'table art'. Selected contributions are mounted and displayed as part of the decor. It's a pleasure to take the children to these restaurants.

**Moral:** Details overlooked by the competition can often provide a competitive edge.

**Car hire**

Early one Saturday morning I called to rent a car. At the end of thirty rings, I hung up. (Maybe they're not yet open.) I try again a little later. Finally, the operator answers and says, 'I'm going to find someone to take care of you,' I wait a good five minutes, after which I give up. The competition took good care of me.

**Moral:** It is not enough to have a big name and a big fleet to be successful in the car rental business.

**The airport**

There is a sign at the airport at the entrance to the railway station saying: 'Welcome to the United Kingdom'. On this particular day, abandoned empty trolleys outnumber luggage-carrying passengers. Trolleys are not allowed down onto the platforms as they might roll onto the track. (No-one thought to invest in trolleys that automatically brake and need to be released by users.) The chaos at the ticket counter and ticket barrier was unbelievable as passengers struggled to get through. Two British Rail employees stood watching the melee. They obviously did not consider it their job to move the trolleys. When I pointed out the irony of the welcome sign and the chaotic scene below it, one of them replied: 'We did not ask you to come here, did we?'

**Moral:** A welcome consists of more than just a welcome sign.

**The vet**

A friend took her Siberian Husky to the veterinarian. She suspected that the dog had a fractured leg. Since it was not possible for her to leave the office early, the vet agreed to stay late in order to treat 'Nikko'. The leg was indeed broken. Nikko's leg was splinted and he was given a mild sedative. Friend and dog did not leave the vet's office until nearly 10 pm.

The next morning the doctor called to check on Nikko's condition, recommended ways to guarantee his comfort for the coming day and offered his home phone number should any further difficulties arise.

**Moral:** Sometimes dogs get treated better than humans.

**A Mercedes dealer**

I went to a Mercedes dealer, having decided to acquire an automobile whose reputation we all know.

A salesman is talking to me, but interrupts himself each time a new customer comes in. At the end of several interruptions, I leave exasperated. Obviously, I did not buy the Mercedes.

**Moral:** One does not sell a service with a 'good morning sir'.

**Expired MOT**

I confess. I was recently stopped for driving while my MOT had expired. I received a summons to appear in court at 10 am on the last Thursday in September. Unfortunately, I had to be out of town the entire last week of the month, and moreover, the designated law courts were an hour's drive from both my home and office.

I checked with my insurance company to see if the violation would increase my premiums. I'm informed that my offence is a minor one and that the charge is usually dropped upon presentation of a receipt proving that the car had been inspected.

Next, I phoned the courts. Yes, the offence is considered a minor one. No, I cannot have the court date changed (since the offence is SO minor). Yes, expired-MOT charges are usually dropped, but only at the discretion of the arresting officer. His work number should be on my warrant.

The officer is difficult to reach as he's generally on his beat. Finally, he returned my call. Yes, he would be happy to recommend that my charge be dropped. No, he will not assume responsibility for remembering our conversation. If I can find him at the courts, he will recommend dropping charges. (But a trip to the courts is what I've been trying to avoid all along.)

It is now the last Monday in September. I call the court office and explain my plight. The lady suggested that I drive to the court house and pay the fine and court costs. (Has no one been listening?) Yes, there is an alternative. I can mail the payment, but it must be processed before 10 am on Thursday.

I hurry to the post office. I xerox a copy of my inspection receipt and send it with a check for the proper amount. I'm assured that it will be delivered no later than Wednesday. Just to make sure, I also sent it Registered.

Two weeks later, I received a bill from the court asking for more money. I was tried (in absentia) and found guilty. That means I owe an extra £25. What happened?

I call the court clerk. She takes 10 minutes to find the records of my case. Yes, my check was received. Yes, it is noted that the correspondence was sent Registered and it arrived at 4:30PM on Wednesday. Unfortunately, one of the clerks was getting married Thursday morning and being short-handed, the remaining staff did not post the late Wednesday mail until noon on Thursday. I was scheduled to be in court at 10 am. That's why I was found guilty in my absence and fined an extra $25.

**Moral:** For my next book, I will consider adding 'marriage of clerks' as a factor in determining service quality.

**Credit cards**

My wife and I had separate credit card accounts. One day, while paying bills, I noticed that both payments were to be sent to an identical office. I wrote one check and noted the amounts that were to be credited to each of the accounts (including account numbers). I made a similar notation in the proper space on each of the billing slips. I enclosed the two billing slips and the check in the same envelope and sent them off.

A week later I received a phone call demanding that I make a payment on my card. I explained what I had done and was told: 'You cannot do that! That's not the way the system is set up. We cannot credit two accounts from the same check. That would be too complicated.'

Not wishing to make life too complicated for the credit card system, I paid off both accounts and soon received a set of brand new cards from the competition.

**Moral**: Company-friendly (as opposed to customer-friendly) accounting systems lose customers.

**The electricity company**

Most New Yorkers would prefer to spar with Mike Tyson than deal with the electricity company. That fact made a colleague's recent experience all the more remarkable.

She called their office to get electricity connected for an apartment she intended to lease for her business. The account executive who was assigned the call was exceptionally helpful. First, he suggested that if she listed the apartment in her own name the rates would be considerably cheaper than if she listed it as a business property. After admitting that the apartment building did not fall into his sector, he provided the name and extension number of the person who would be responsible. He asked a few more questions and suggested a few short-cuts to expediting the process. Finally, he invited my colleague 'to get back to him' if anything was unnecessarily delayed.

The colleague was stunned. This from the electricity company?

**Moral:** Service quality can sometimes be found where you least expect it.

**The 10 am news**

They're talking about the marathon and there certainly is one. My car is blocked on a one-way street in the middle of the city. Dwelling on the details of the race, the sportscaster is covering everything from the colour of the sweatsuits to the leg muscle movements. Naturally, nothing is mentioned about how to bypass the resulting traffic jam. But to whom is the sportscaster speaking? To the other automobile drivers stuck on this street? It is probable that they are grumbling just as much as I am. To marathon fans? They are already occupied as they are probably in the race or in the stands. The station must be convinced that there are many interested listeners at home in their armchairs.

**Moral:** Someone at the radio station needs to define the 'target clientele' for the 10 am news.

**Le Concorde and Manhattan taxies**

I am flying to New York for a business meeting. Since I'm short on time, I spend the extra money to fly Concorde. Concorde is generally used by businessmen. It is not surprising to find the passenger list entirely comprised of males.

A short time before landing, passengers are presented with a toilet kit so that they might freshen up a bit. When the flight attendant reached my seat, she informed me that I would receive a set of women's toilet articles. They had run out of men's toilet kits. Run out? Men comprise over 90 per cent of their business. How could they run out? I was a 'dissatisfied' customer.

In order to reach my meeting, I flagged a New York taxi. New York cabbies have a reputation for being tough and insensitive. My driver was a pleasant surprise. He understood that I was running late and drove accordingly. When we were approaching my destination, he took care to ask which side of the avenue would be more convenient. (It was raining and he noted that de-cabbing on the wrong side of the street might incur a 2 minute wait for a light change).

The cabbie received a handsome tip.

**Moral:** Price is not always a guarantee of service quality.

**The Chernobyl disaster – cultural differences**

While no word at all from French authorities was reaching the French, all the Japanese embassies and consulates received instructions to invite Japanese citizens abroad to go to their offices for an information session to provide advice about health and food.

**Moral:** There are public services which actually provide service to the public.

**A good insurance story**

I had a crack in my windshield. I remember the morning when a stone from a gravel truck cracked it. The crack seems to get longer every day.

A friend suggested that most windshield problems are covered standard by auto insurance policies.

I called the insurance company. Yes, the company would replace my windshield. I was given a number to call to make an appointment, and supplied with a code number to expedite the glass company's paper work.

The glass company offered me two choices: I could bring the car to them for the replacement, or they would send a service truck and do the job at my home. I chose the latter. The glass man arrived punctually. He carefully scraped my state and city stickers from the old windshield. He then installed the new one, re-applied the decals and concluded his visit by washing all the windows in the car.

**Moral:** The statistics may have to be revised. I have now told hundreds of people about my pleasant experience.

**My neighbourhood bookshop**

A friend recently opened a bookshop. He's doing marvellously well. He says he sells books. Yes, he does. Actually he delivers a superior service quality to people interested in books.

He makes it a point to welcome every new customer to the shop. He explains how his operation works, while taking you on a tour of the facility. The customer gives him vital information: name, address, phone and general/specific reading/collecting interests. He prepares bi-monthly mailings, listing titles in stock and the ones due to arrive in the next 30 days. One is invited to order ahead.

Every month he lists at least one book, whose author will make an appearance at the store.

On Sunday afternoons, he encourages interested people to join him for an informal discussion of some especially interesting book. The bookseller provides refreshments.

During the holidays, he offers a special line of 'gift books' so that book lovers can do their best to convert friends. Since 'gift books' might mean converts, they sell at 20 per cent off list. Of course, gift wrapping is free.

Saturday mornings are set aside for children. Parents are invited to bring the children into the shop and read to them, or let them read themselves, from the children's book section. Children's size chairs are provided, along with hot chocolate and apple juice for refreshments. (It always amazes me how many of those children's books find homes on Saturday morning.)

**Moral:** More shops like this and Gutenberg could once more become a very popular guy in my neighbourhood.

**Public transport**

I have a meeting in Northampton on Tuesday morning. My train to Northampton is due to leave from Euston at 9.20 am. With time to spare I set off from my home in North London to my usual BR station. First hurdle: the train I intended taking has been cancelled due to staff shortage. With still time to spare I wait for the next one and end up in Finsbury Park, from where I plan taking the Victoria line to Euston. A Victoria line train appears; I get on it. We arrive at Highbury & Islington, the train stops, the doors open, and . . . never close again! It gets warmer and warmer in the train and everybody is wondering why we're not moving. Then, after a good 15 minutes, it is announced: ' . . . all change. This train terminates here'. Resigned, we shuffle onto the platform, hoping that another train will appear soon. At the end of yet another 15 minutes, we're informed that '. . . due to a fire in the tunnels, there will be no train southbound until further notice.' Did they not know about this fire when we first pulled into the station? If so, could they not have told us straight away, and given me the chance to make it to Euston by taxi? As it was, I had to cancel my meeting in Northampton and arrange a new one. Does give a good impression, doesn't it?

**Moral:** A little bit of information earlier one would have done a great deal to avoid this disaster.

**My new chairs - 31 December**

I've purchased some new furniture from an up-market retailer. They deliver. They'll call and tell me when. Finally the call comes: my furniture will be delivered on December 31. They cannot tell me what time. It is up to me to hang around. Three days before the 31st, they notify me that they're unable to deliver part of my order on time. I would have to wait two weeks longer for the table, but the chairs will be delivered. The long-awaited day finally arrives. I would have chairs for my New Year's Eve party!

But fortune frowns on me. At 9 am, I discover that the apartment building interphone is out of order. Have the delivery people already come and gone? Yes! I call the store to propose some possible solutions . . . all rejected with no appeal:

– 'Can you notify the deliverymen?'
– 'Impossible. No radio in the truck.'
– 'Can I call them at the next customer's place?'
– 'Impossible. Cannot give out customer's addresses.'
– 'Could you call them yourself, at the next customer's place?'
– 'Impossible. We cannot bother our customers.'

And to add to my great joy, they explain to me that the deliverymen are going to keep their truck for New Year's Eve so, according to them, my furniture might be stolen in the meantime. I ask for a new delivery date. Only the delivery manager is authorized to give a date. He's at the doctor's office and will not be back until Monday. I ask for the sales manager. He tells me that only the President has the right to order a delivery schedule shorter than the regular one. Bad luck again, he has gone off skiing.

In desperation, I rent a truck and pick up the furniture at the warehouse.

Do I have to tell you how long it was until the tables were finally delivered? Of course, there was no sign of a letter of apology for either situation.

**Moral:** The furniture business must be in pretty good shape.

Enough! I believe I've made my point. Since my story notebook is full, maybe, one day I'll write another book: a bible about sure ways to lose (or win) customers. As you have seen, there are no shortage of ways.

## Self-diagnosis

- Prepare your own 'blunder book' for one month, noting all the happy and sad moments in your daily life.
- Ask the people who use your services to do the same thing.
- What are the lessons which you draw from your company?
- A new opening or opportunity? A new segment to attack?
- Improve your standards? Your service delivery system?
- Improve your error chase?

# 10

# How to Launch a Service Quality Programme

By now, you know that the customer always wants better service quality. You also know that his conception of quality is not necessarily the same as yours. You have already decided to compete with a policy of service quality rather than declare a price war. How do you now start a service quality programme in your company? You know that there's room for improvement, but you have a lot of questions:

- Does the quality promise match market expectations?
- Is the quality promise clearly formulated? Is it usable from the top to the bottom of the organization?
- Is the promise competitive? Is it adequately communicated to potential customers?
- Are there quality standards? If so, are they measurable? Are they known to everyone in the company? Does the service delivered conform to the standards?
- Does the service match the identified level of excellence?
- Is it in the implementation stage that the quality slips?
- Is the customer content? What else can be done for the customer to maintain a competitive advantage?

To answer these questions, there is only one thing to do: Ask the customer! Run a survey. Use interviews and questionnaires. This will enable you to continually monitor all the people upon whom the success of your company depends.

Find out what your customers want. What are their needs? How can they be served? What is the competition doing? If there are no similar products, look at what is being done in analogous sectors. If you want to design a computer repair service procedure, look at what appliance or typewriter repair people are doing. Above all, do not forget the employees who are in direct contact with the customers. They know plenty!

What you learn from the customer will enable you to diagnose the health of your service. The resultant diagnosis should specify whether you must completely rethink your quality policy, or whether you must improve it with some fine tuning

## Diagnosis, the inevitable starting point

Is the service quality problem the accumulation of errors all along the chain? Is the service promise always kept? Is quality too much in the hands of the front-line supervisor, the store managers, the delivery or the repair staff? Does quality vary from one location to another? How? Is the competition catching up? How? All of these questions are part of a proper service quality diagnosis.

Yet putting too much faith in the instruments used in the diagnosis can be a mistake. Most banks do not directly survey customer satisfaction. They merely track the number of accounts closed and the degree of activity in the remaining accounts. These two performance indicators will never tell them why an account has been closed or become inactive.

Diagnosis is the keystone of any quality programme. It will tell the manager whether he must initiate an error chase to try for zero-defect, or whether he must give the quality strategy a complete review.

A diagnosis is always more difficult for a market leader. The leader often prefers to rest on his laurels. Due to lack of vigilance, the quality of his service slowly deteriorates. It takes courage to react and accept change. The market leader needs more alarm signals than others, because there is always a lag between service shortcomings and falling sales, and the leader's self-image plays against him. It can mask his faults.

The customer may also be more lenient. He assumes that the leader knows best. (After all, that's why he's the leader.) That is, until the day he suddenly takes his business to the competition. To the leader's dismay, the customer may have discovered a better, less expensive alternative.

The Number 1 position in itself, may be a handicap. Many customers are suspicious of the leader, prejudging his arrogance and preferring to do business with someone who may be more appreciative. The Japanese have used this behaviour to their

advantage. Penetrating markets from the bottom, they surround their products with superior service. They nibble away at local competitors and finally take over the market with a superior product and service quality. The day when they will be able to dominate insurance, banking and chain retailing is on the way. In less than a decade, Japanese banks have become the world's largest.

Self-diagnosis is always difficult when everything is going well. After all, 'What is the hassle?' How do restaurant chains such as TGIF motivate their staff to do better when the place is always packed? Why work harder when all the tables are occupied, when people are being turned away and when the restaurant is even doing well at off-peak times?

To know whether a diagnosis is valid, it may be necessary to ask whether it answers three questions: Is the quality level good? Is the quality level respected? Finally, is it better than the competition?

## In quest of zero-defect

Small quality errors are the most difficult to track down. They are generally far from the home office; on the customer's premises, in the various stores of a chain, or in other countries. They might also be happening 24 hours a day. Some aspects of a service are better than the competition. In others, the competition may have the lead. Eliminating these small service errors is the responsibility of everyone in the organization.

Maintaining the level of excellence everywhere/at all times is a fundamental job. In fact, it must become an obsession. It is not enough to create a service Quality Control Department.

Quality circles and the participation of staff in direct contact with the customers will be particularly effective. Every initiative will help to avoid or correct errors, and hence to perfect the quality structure.

The error chase must be an all-consuming discipline. It is not just a question of method.

Employees must be taught to be proud to do it right first time. Little victories must be rewarded. Quality circles must meet often and regularly. On average, a quality circle will produce about twenty perceptible improvements. These little improvements will directly influence the customer's judgment.

All the quality champions apply the same rule; it is better to try to improve one hundred details by one per cent than to try for 100 per cent progress on a single aspect of service. Only systematic effort produces tangible results. A quest for zero-defect cannot be improvised. Here are the main steps:

1. *Make sure that the quality standards are shared by everyone.* It is useless to ask someone to do it right first time if he does not know exactly what to do. Standards must be clear and specific. They must also match your promise. (Sometimes they have to be re-specified for the various parts of the organization.) They must be understood by all the people concerned. (A service company employing ten thousand people, must create from one thousand to three thousand standards, dependent upon the complexity of the service.) Assess the work to be accomplished and the time it will take to communicate clear standards to the employees.

2. *Define the priorities.* An error chase must not run off in all directions. It is essential that the chase be conducted with clearly stated priorities. What comes first? The welcome? Response speed? Service time? Complaint handling? Cleanliness?

   The diagnosis should provide an order of priorities. Another approach is to attack the pressing problems first and to plan more comprehensively after the brush fires have been extinguished.

   This approach may not be suitable for companies having little or no familiarity with the philosophy of total quality. If the error chase is limited to only a single department, major successes will be difficult to achieve. Companies adopting the error chase for the first time need to launch a generalized campaign, beginning with the top management. In order to be able to evaluate results quickly, it may be a good idea to choose a test site where a quality programme is run and compare its performance with that of an equivalent site.

3. *Launching a zero-defect campaign for all levels of personnel.* Once priorities are established, it is necessary to mobilize enthusiasm. A company-wide gathering will get everyone on the bandwagon. This is only a first step, but one that is indispensable to altering the company culture and to orienting everyone toward the customer.

The decision to strive for zero-defect does not guarantee success. A company-wide communication effort will be necessary. Speeches, posters, emblems, audiovisuals, diplomas, badges, prizes, contests, logos, and slogans can each play a role.

Everything must be carefully organized. And remember, it is very difficult to attain zero-defect. Perfection is not of this world!

4. *Training for the chase for zero-defect.* The success of an error-chase depends on two factors: knowledge of the quality standards and the ability of the groups to work together. Teams must be trained to deal with both points. Seminars with the correct mix of information and discussion must be planned at regular intervals. The entire organization must be represented. It is preferable to hold the seminars within the firm rather than to send people outside. There is not a lot of literature on the subject. Most of the available documentation concerns product quality. Furthermore, 'home-made' work-shops and seminars symbolize top management's commitment to improve service quality, and data specific to the company will be available.

5. *Setting up an error chase procedure.* The error chase procedure is organized around two mechanisms: the establishment of the work groups, and the information feedback which will be implemented. The sooner employees can observe the tangible effects of the error-chase, the more they will be motivated to continue the work.

   Firms, which have continual contact with the customer, should be certain to integrate the customer into the process. Hotels, department stores, restaurants, transportation facilities, hospitals, schools, banks, telecommunications companies, sports and leisure activities are all 'worlds' where the presence of the client in the working groups is indispensable.

6. *Measure the progress accomplished and spread the word.* It is necessary to measure the effects of the proposed actions with regard to the clientele and to communicate the results throughout the organization as soon as possible. For this purpose, the bulletin board and the newsletter are indispensable. Do not forget to mention all the little victories in official speeches.

## Bringing the service rendered into question

The quality diagnosis may conclude that there is a mismatch between the service rendered and the customer's expectations. In this case, it is less important to track down errors than to bring the service promise into question. Quality circles will not work. Only a thorough rethinking by general management can restructure a quality strategy. It can be done, as the following example shows!

> Club Med recently realized that the expectations of German, Italian and British holidaymakers were not the same as those of the French, who constituted its traditional market. The Club first tried to satisfy everybody with a series of minor adjustments in the villages. Result: no one was satisfied.
>
> The CEO at the time, Serge Trigano, then saw two possibilities: design a new product, the international village, or arrange the villages by nationality and promote them in the appropriate countries.
>
> He chose the first approach. Seventeen villages were selected. They were taken out of the brochure aimed at the French market, and promoted separately to the 'Europeans'.
>
> In these villages, the welcome and reception were re-thought to take into account the full range of arrivals and departures. The buffet table added a variety of dishes including specialties from the various European countries. The GOs were asked to speak several languages. Very quickly, the satisfaction index of the Germans, Italians, Belgians and British rose by 20 per cent.

While the error chase is conducted from the bottom to the top of an organization, restructuring of the service strategy must come from the top. Employees in direct contact with the customer can signal behaviour which indicates dissatisfaction, but they cannot redesign strategies. They do not possess an overall view, nor do they have the data necessary to make broad policy decisions. General management must decide whether it will be preferable to try out a new strategy on a pilot site or to implement it throughout the company. However, since front-line people have the best opportunity to observe customer reactions, it is always wise to include them in the decision making.

Employee communications must be written with considerable care. It is more difficult to get a radically new, management-proposed approach accepted than it is to spread the results of a zero-defect chase.

Serge Trigano brought together all the GOs of his Europe/Africa sector, in groups of fifty, when he unveiled his new service strategy. A welcome book was distributed to new, non-French GOs to familiarize them with Club Med culture. The participants were soon sold on the new strategy.

The campaign clearly demonstrated the importance that management attached to the new villages. Nevertheless, it made sure that sales people would not designate these new villages as 'purgatories', advising the French against them. It positioned them as 'unique occasions' to get out of the French shell.

There are barometers which suggest that a service needs re-tooling. The best sign is a steady drop in the customer satisfaction rate. One must be doubly suspect when, after having rectified a number of service elements, the rate continues to drop. The competition must also be constantly monitored. Any drop in market share means that customers are going elsewhere. Finally, no satisfaction rating (even 98 per cent) is secure if the competition's rate is getting closer. One's competitive advantage may be slipping!

At the beginning of the 1980s, Singapore Airlines found itself in such a situation. Cathay Pacific was the competition. Until then, Singapore Airlines, according to its own surveys and those of international aviation, was Number 1 in its region. Cathay Pacific began by imitating Singapore Airlines. Gradually, it innovated, nibbling away at the market share.

Complaint letters sent to Singapore Airlines dealt with little things. Passengers were not happy with baggage services (usually at airports where baggage handling was sub-contracted) or noted that crew enthusiasm seemed to be slipping. (The drop in enthusiasm may have been the result of frequent personnel transfers.)

Singapore Airlines had two options. It could address the questions raised by the passengers, or, step back and re-examine its total service programme. The first path would merely mean improving baggage control and stimulating a fresh team spirit among flight personnel. The second path would mean inventing new services to counter Cathay Pacific. Singapore Airlines opted for the latter and introduced seats which were convertible for sleeping. (This strategy was later abandoned as a result of a customer survey.) Then it began offering games and a wider choice of films.

Such decisions modify each service chain. By redefining the service strategy, one modifies promises and quality standards. At the same time, it may become necessary to retrain employees, if not replace them. A new advertising campaign may also be necessary.

When Xerox entered the office automation systems business, it set up a new service chain. They could not use photocopy machine salespeople and repair staff to serve microcomputer customers. From the operational management to information policy, everything was designed to respond to the new activity, including the customer satisfaction indicators.

## A shared trunk of excellence for several service branches

A company frequently serves several market segments. For each of them, it will need an appropriate quality policy plus a programme for chasing errors or re-evaluating total service delivery. A travel agency, for example, can address itself to tourists and to businessmen. Two different emphases, two different sets of needs, two different quality policies. However, the agency can only succeed in both markets by developing a shared trunk of excellence upon which the service branches are grafted. It will also need a homogeneous policy of high quality for welcome, telephone answering, office decoration and staff know-how.

Another example is the auto parts dealer who serves several customer market segments. It may serve a small repair garage which can only stock a minimum parts inventory and needs frequent deliveries. It may also serve a large garage which wants efficient invoicing, inventory counseling and volume pricing. A third customer may be a delivery firm which manages its own truck fleet. It often needs maintenance assistance and/or repair service. Although each segment benefits from a specific service, it must be linked to the others by a shared trunk which will provide perfect quality conformity. At IBM France, a total service quality policy dominates all the segments. It is organized around four concepts:

- a quality definition, shared by all,
- preventive maintenance planning (favoured mode of action),
- quality measurement, generalized throughout the company, and
- zero-defect.

Total quality management is founded on three management principles:

- top management commitment,
- employee commitment (with priority given to teamwork) and,
- a rational approach to improving quality.

A quality committee, chaired by the CEO of IBM France, meets once a month. Quality plans are integrated in the strategic planning. Performance evaluation takes into account the results achieved by quality actions. Quality circles and progress groups exist on a permanent basis. All client relations are codified with accurate measurement of deviations. Once a compliance deviation appears, an error chase is launched. From 1982 to 1985, the number of working groups, which met for approximately one hour per week, grew from two hundred and thirty to approximately nine hundred.

# Conclusion

As a conclusion, I am sure you will not be surprised if I ask you to participate in a satisfaction survey. Naturally, I gathered together a number of readers in order to learn what questions to ask. They also helped me measure the 'quality' perceived by the reader, and the 'quality' imagined by the author. So I shall not ask you if you like the form or the sequencing logic. The qualitative survey reveals that you could not care less. In spite of everything, if certain questions seem valueless to you, do not hesitate to check the block labeled 'silly question'. Satisfaction cannot be measured on a large scale unless it is simple for the customer to respond. The questionnaire on pages 105 and 106 is to be sent to the address shown at the top of page 105.

Thank you in advance for your cooperation dear customer-reader, and perhaps 'see you soon' if this book satisfies you.

# Bibliography


Albrecht K., Zemke R., *Service America,* Hollywood, Illinois, Dow Jones - Irwin, 1985

Bloch Ph., Ababou R., Xardel D., *Service Compris,* Paris, Hachette l'Expansion, 1986

De Bruicker F.S., Summe G.L., 'Make Customers Keep Coming Back', *Harvard Business Review*, January-February 1985

Hart C.W.L., Casserly G.D., 'Quality, a Brand New, Tested Strategy', *The Cornell HRA Quarterly,* November 1985

Ingle S. & N., *Quality Circles in Service Industries,* Englewood Cliffs, N.J., Prentice-Hall, 1983

Ishikawa K., *La Gestion de la Qualité,* Paris, Dunod, 1985

Jackson B.B., 'Build Customer Relationships that Last', *Harvard Business Review,* November-December 1985

Jones C., De Cotus T.A., 'Video-assisted Selection of Hotel Employees', *The Cornell HRA Quarterly,* August 1986

Juran J.M., *Gestion de la Qualite*, Normes et Techniques, AFNOR, 1983

Levitt T., 'Marketing Success Through Differentiation – of Anything', *Harvard Business Review,* January-February 1980

Levitt T., 'Marketing Intangible Products and Product Intangibles', *Harvard Business Review,* May-June 1981

Lewis R.C., 'The Positioning Statement for Hotels', *The Cornell HRA Quarterly,* May 1981

Lovelock C.H., *Service Marketing,* Englewood Cliffs, N.J. Prentice-Hall, 1984

Monteil B. et al., *Les Outils des Cercles et l'Amelioration de la Qualité,* Paris, Les Editions d'Organisation, 1985

Peters T., Austin N., *La Passion de l'Excellence*, Paris, InterEditions, 1985,

Sasser W.E., Olsen R.P., Wycoff D., *Management of Service Operations,* Boston, Allyn and Bacon, 1978

Sele M.M., Karmarkar U.S., 'Good Product Support is Smart Marketing'., *Harvard Business Review,* November-December 1983

Stora G., Montaigne J., *La Qualité totale dans l'Entreprise*, Paris, Les Editions d'Organisation, March 1986

# Questionnaire

Please complete the following questionnaire and send to:

J. Horovitz
MSR
BP 78
1, Place Royale
F-78102 St Germain-en-Laye
FRANCE

| | *yes* | *no* | *silly question* |
|---|---|---|---|
| Are you generally satisfied with this book? | | | |
| Does it keep its title's promise? | | | |
| Does it match the promise of its advertising? | | | |
| **THANKS TO THIS BOOK:** | | | |
| Have you been able to perform a diagnosis of your firm's service quality? | | | |
| Have you determined three action priorities for service quality for the next year? | | | |
| Has there been some fundamental change in your way of thinking about your quality? | | | |

Have you solved – on paper anyway – at least one service quality problem which you could not solve before?

Do you feel that you have acquired a clear and accurate method for approaching service quality in your company?

How many extra customers do you think you will gain thanks to this approach?

How many customers do you think you will keep thanks to this approach?

In your opinion, what chapter(s) deserved to be developed further?
In your opinion, what chapter(s) is / (are) too long?

What chapter(s) do you find to be useless?

THANK YOU FOR YOUR HELP!

So that we can get to know each other a bit better, could I also have the following information?

- What's your firm's primary function?

- Number of employees in your company?

0 to 49 50 to 99 100 to 499 500 to 999 1000 to 1999 2000 and +

- Your position?

CEO/President Middle Management Supervisor Customer Contact Personnel

- Your department?

ADMINISTRATION Marketing Sales After-sales service Financial Other

THANK YOU AGAIN!

**Management in Service Industries**
Edited by Peter Jones

This impressive collection of original articles from leaders in the fields of management education and service sector management provides an excellent overview of new research and practice in this growing area of the economy.

The book has three key objectives:

- to review current approaches to the management of services industries
- to identify characteristics of the different sectors of the service industry
- to analyse the impact these have on service operations.

An informative and stimulating guide to future trends in strategic management in the service sector, the book is essential reading for all those interested in management development in a fast-developing and international industrial sector.

Published 1989, 326 pages, Paper, ISBN 0 273 02953 3
Also available in hardback

**A Communication Audit Handbook**
**Helping Organizations Communicate**
S C Hamilton

Effective communication is now recognised as a crucial factor in the success of a business. The first step in developing a first class communication system is to implement a communication audit, i.e. an appraisal of present lines of communication needs and a report on how these needs can be met.

This handbook is a practical up-to-date guide to commissioning and conducting such an audit. It will be of use to general managers who are commissioning communications agencies who conduct audits, PR consultants undertaking communication audits for the first time and students of marketing, public relations and corporate communications.

The book contains three sample communication audits and a log book compiled by an auditor for a fictional organisation.

Published 1987, 208 pages, Cased, ISBN 0 273 02829 4

**Managing Employee Absence for a Competitive Edge**
Andrzej Huczynski and Michael Fitzpatrick

Millions of pounds are lost in industry and commerce each year through employee absence. The cost includes not only sick pay and overtime expenses but additional, consequential costs such as unnecessarily high manning levels, lost production and orders, disruptions and shutdown of sections and low morale among company employees. Clearly, understanding, controlling and reducing absence offers major opportunities to improve productivity, quality and service.

This book is designed as a starting point for all managers keen to increase profits by effective control of employee absence.

Drawing on international research, statistics and case studies, the authors begin by defining absence and uncovering the multitude of problems it creates. Next, the book addresses the diverse causes of absence and shows how managers can isolate absence problems in their own companies and develop an effective control programme.

Published 1989, 288 pages, Papers, ISBN 0 273 02850 2

**Achieving Results Through Time Management**
Philip Atkinson

Philip Atkinson's guide to the efficient use of working time is designed for the manager or self-starter who wants to excel and develop the new skills of the effective executive.

Achieving Results Through Time Management is more than an introduction to time management, it is a compendium which staff at all levels will find of interest and value.

Highlighting both the key activities of managerial and administrative work, the text examines time management problems in many different ways. The emphasis is on isolating the key areas of time wastage, planning a more effective working day and on actually putting the plan into action.

Includes chapers on:

- Planning, problem solving, procrastination and assertiveness which will be useful for staff members who find that there is not enough time in the day to achieve their key results.

- Career and stress management to help the manager who is working under the pressure of constant innovation.
- Problem solving, reading and writing skills, meetings, management and delegation are all covered. Overall, the book provides managers with a wealth of information which can be used to improve their performance.

Published 1988, 192 pages, Cased, ISBN 0 273 02733 6

**Beyond the Great Divide**
**Introducing equality into the company**
Jane Beck and Maggie Steel

More organisations are realising the benefits of introducing equal opportunity programmes as a way of improving the training and development of the whole workforce. Demographic trends leading towards skill shortages, increased flexible working and recent legislation will encourage equal opportunities further.

This book is written for managers wishing to implement effective equal opportunity programmes for women within their organisations. It covers all aspects of the subject including getting commitment for the programmes, sources of help, women returning to work, appraisal, training, monitoring, networking, and future trends. Throughout this book the authors draw on examples and case studies of good practice among companies and public sector organisations.

Published 1989, 192 pages, Paper, ISBN 0 273 03115 5

These books are available in all major bookstores. In case of difficulty, the books may be ordered from: Southport Book Distributors, 12-14 Slaidburn Crescent, Fylde Road, Southport PR9 9YF United Kingdom
Tel: 0704 26881